sukumarnayar@yahoo.ca

ISBN:1-4609-3631-0

ISBN-13:978-1-4609-3631-3

LCCN:2011903197

THE VIVID AIR

A Memoir

SUKUMAR NAYAR

This book is dedicated to
three people who matter most in my life:
my wife, Nalini
my son, Nikku
my daughter, Radha

The unexamined life is not worth living.

−Socrates

CONTENTS

PREFACE

The circumstances leading up to the effort of writing this book are described elsewhere. After reading the first draft, I was still wondering if there is a readership out there. I was also wondering if the anecdotes and episodes that I had selected for inclusion provide the best possible reading experience. Truth be told, I have many, many more stories to tell. However, for fear of making the book unwieldy, I had to limit the number of anecdotes. It was a struggle.

The format was another issue. Somehow I disliked a straight chronology of events. I know that this is not an ordinary tale, and so I argued that it deserves a special format. I have warned the readers early in the book that the treatment will offend sequence and throw chronology out of the window.

I must say that it has been a labor of love and that I am glad I "succumbed" to my daughter's encouragement to document my life. Here, again, I was faced with a dilemma. Do I talk about my extensive travel around the world? Do I talk about my professional accomplishments as a teacher and administrator? Or do I write about my experience in theatre as a director, actor, and dramaturge?

In the end, the manuscript turned out to be skirting around all of them, meaning that I had not delved into any one of them deeply.

It has also been difficult to pick suitable or relevant photographs from the several dozen albums and files. Every photograph has a story to tell; each document stands witness to some incident!

Again, I had to be wary of space restrictions.

Also, I had to make a calculated decision to omit writing about my somewhat large, extended family. My father had many cousins, who in turn, had many children of their own. I have lost count, but I suspect there are/were more than twenty-five. Also, I ought to have included the many cousins, nephews, and nieces from my wife's side. My many pleasant experiences involving them and my relationship with all of them are, perhaps, material for another book.

I did agonize over a suitable title. I looked at many biographies and autobiographies. First, I thought of something goofy like Alan Alda's memoir, *Never Have Your Dog Stuffed: And Other Things I've Learned*. I toyed with *Beyond Middleclass*. Finally, I decided on *The Vivid Air*, inspired by a quote that appears elsewhere in the book.

When the manuscript was with the Editor, I was browsing Amazon for books and to my astonishment I noticed that there are three other books under the same name *The Vivid Air*, even though they did not belong to the genre of memoirs! Copyright issues raised their collective heads, but the Publisher allayed my fears and said that I am not in violation of any laws. So I decided to keep the title because it has a certain ring to it. The Editor enthusiastically concurred with this sentiment as well.

S.N.
Toronto, Canada
May, 2011

CHAPTER ONE

WHAT'S IN A NAME?
PLENTY, IF YOU ARE AN INDIAN

It is Tuesday April 27, 2010. Around 3:00 p.m. I decided that I should write a memoir of sorts, something my family and many of my friends have been asking me to do for quite some time.

So, why now?

My daughter was driving me somewhere, and I mentioned in passing that when I was a student in London, I had known E. R. Braithwaite the author of *To Sir, With Love.*

"I didn't know that," my daughter exclaimed.

Then, for the umpteenth time, she said, "You know, Daddy, you *have* to write these things down. We know very little about you, your childhood, things you have done, people you have met, and so on, except snippets that occasionally come out of your mouth."

As I said, this demand had come from many sources. I suppose what prompted these people to keep on encouraging me was that, during a very long and eventful career, I have had the opportunity to meet a lot of people—some of them very well known in their chosen field of activity—and had the great fortune to travel to many countries, witness interesting events, sometimes getting into scrapes, receiving kudos from many sources...

So, whenever I shared my experiences with people, they would, invariably, suggest that I document them.

Looking back, what I see is an amorphous mass of experiences and "information", and if I were to settle down to give it some shape, I need to conceptualize a format and, at this stage, I admit that I do not have one. Even if I discovered one, I am not quite sure for whom I am writing this. Sure, the members of the family and close friends might enjoy the episodes and escapades; but is there a larger readership? And if not, does it matter? If I get this published, who knows? It just might make its way on to the bestseller list!

But I will go on a limb and say that it is, at the very least, a very *interesting* story.

Certainly there are people out there who have traveled to forty-one countries, people who have stood astride the equator, people who have climbed Kilimanjaro, people who have met or talked to Noam Chomsky, Peter Brook, Helen Hayes, Victor Turner, Richard Schechner (all giants in their respective fields of expertise), people who came close to being incarcerated in a foreign jail because they looked like someone else—say a suspected terrorist—people who had been involved in some capacity or another in over one hundred and fifty stage productions, people who have worked for the United Nations or the Canadian Executive Services Organization, people who speak six or seven languages, people who have held senior administrative positions in the university system...

But if one person has been able to accomplish all this, I submit that it is an interesting life.

There is also, perhaps, a success story—a story of a very ordinary individual, born in a very remote part of the southwestern corner of the vast subcontinent of India, not born to riches or lineage, the story of just one of more than a billion inhabitants of the great country. Success could be a very deceptive term. It is certainly subjective. Success compared to what? And who decides the level of success—whatever that might be? Who decides whether a life has been successful or not?

I must say that I don't have the answers, but I have decided to unwind a complicated reel and to document some of the experiences that contributed to an eventful life.

And since I don't have a template for autobiographies, you are forewarned that this narrative will crisscross continents, will offend chronology and sequence. The hope is that you end up with some sort of a shape to, what I have already mentioned is, an amorphous mass that is known generally as Sukumar Nayar.

Here is the first interesting point. If the name in my passport is anything to go by, my name should be Parameswaran Sukumaran Nayar. That is also the name by which the Canada Revenue Agency recognizes me.

Let me start with the last name, first. It should be by tradition spelled *"Nair"*. *"Nayar"* is typically a north Indian name. For reasons unbeknownst to me, when I graduated from university, the diploma displayed in fancy, cursive writing that the degree of Bachelor of Science had been awarded to a man whose last name was "Nayar", and thus, I was forced to change the spelling of my last name. Now, you have to remember that when I was growing up, "Nair" was considered a "high caste" Hindu and the community usually frowned upon any tampering with the name. However, my father accepted my new baptism, because the alternative would have been to go through massive bureaucratic maneuvers, and Indians have been for a long time vying with other countries to be the worst bureaucrats in the world. But then, they have the British to thank for that. It is a widely accepted belief that the British left three legacies when they handed over the government to the Indians—cricket, railways, and bureaucracy!

More on the name. In the Western culture, usually, you have a first name, (John, for example) and a last name (Smith, for example). But in India, depending on where you come from, this clean-cut system of nomenclature does not work. For instance, in certain northern states, if your name is Mohandas, and if your father is Karamchand Gandhi, you will be called Mohandas Karamchand Gandhi. In Bengal, however, they follow the Western style. A person has the given name, followed by the last name (*caste* name), like Satyajit Ray or Rabindranath Tagore. But in certain communities in Kerala (God's Own Country, as the travel guides would have you believe) where I came from, traditions are different. Your name will be *preceded* by your father's name and *followed* by your caste name. Thus you have Parameswaran Sukumaran Nayar. I should also mention that this system does not apply to everyone in Kerala either. For instance, many people have their given names preceded by the name of the village of their origin or the name of the family. Also, many people belonging to the "lower castes" omitted it entirely so as not to leave a door open for discrimination. It was easy to identify the caste of a person from the last name. By the way, among the Nairs, girls have their name preceded by their mother's first name!

I suppose I should thank the Lord for small mercies! If I were born in an upper class Sinhalese family in Sri Lanka, I could conceivably have been known as Uda Walawwe Mahim Bandaralage Chanaka Asanka Welegedara! As it happens, Welegedara is one of their prominent cricketers.

Sukumaran became Sukumar, while I was in Uganda, working for the British Civil Service, because my colleagues found it convenient to shorten it. A few called me just "PS". Later—much later—the Canadians would shorten it further to "Suk". So, after all these incarnations, I remain, yours truly, Sukumar Nayar!

As I have already mentioned, "Nair" is supposed to be a high-caste Hindu. I have to admit that I had been exposed to the social implications of being a Nair when I was growing up. I was born in 1928 in the capital city of the state of Kerala, Trivandrum (recently changed to Thiruvananthapuram). My father was a civil servant, an auditor in the Auditor General's Office, in fact. But he was an avid gardener, as well. He was living with the rest of the family—the joint family system allowed that; but he needed space to grow his garden and, hence, moved to the suburbs. "Boondocks" better described the place. I believe I was three at that time. I don't remember anything of the move, but I do recall a man coming very early in the morning to pick roses and jasmine, which would eventually be made into garlands for festive occasions. Receiving someone special by putting a garland around the neck is an old Indian custom.

We had a lot of space to play on, and the kids from the surrounding houses would gather in our yard. I suspect they came also to receive a gift of caramelized banana chips, which my mother had in plentiful supply. But as I grew older, I also noticed that some of the kids did not come inside the house, whereas some others did. I also recall that, when I questioned my parents about this, they said that so and so was from such and such a caste and could not enter the house. I must say that I did not quite understand what it was all about, though I believe I felt something was wrong—seriously wrong. And I don't think I paid much attention to this, until I went to high school. Rather, I should say that I did not think about the *implications* of this, until I went to high school. And when I did, I was quite disturbed, because many of my friends were from "lower" castes, and I could not bring them home; but I didn't think I could do much about the issue. I was not going to start a social upheaval of any kind.

However, someone else did. I want to remind you that I am referring to my native state only. In the early 1950s, a man called Mannath Padmanabhan Pillay (Mannath was not his father's name, but his family name) started a major social reformation by choosing to officially remove his last name Pillay (Pillays are Nairs, as are Menons, Kurups, Thampis, and Panikkars), and many people followed suit. The result was that without the last name, it was not possible to determine the caste of a person. Padmanabhan is a Hindu, and that is all. He could belong to any caste—high or low. This would turn out to be a major revolution in the social history of Kerala.[1]

But I chose to stick with convention. It would have been a huge hassle to attempt to change official records.

I shall never forget the day I was leaving for Uganda to join the British Civil Service. It was in early 1955, and one of my neighbors, a prosperous merchant but of a 'lower' caste, came to say good-bye and gave me a gold ring as a farewell gift. It had a very special design. The head had the symbol of the Indian government carved on it. But this man stood outside the house and gave me the ring through the window. I suppose no one would

---

[1] I must mention that largely due to the influence of Bollywood movies, beginning in the early seventies, many non-Hindu parents had started giving traditionally Hindu names to their children. I suspect that in another fifty years or so, it will be somewhat difficult to identify the caste of a person from the name alone. At least, I hope so!

have prevented him from entering the house. He did not enter, by choice, for fear of offending the social customs.

I still have the ring; when it wears out, I get it remade. After fifty-six years, there is still some of the old gold left in it.

I do want to stress at this time that, in India, the Nairs were not the only community that practiced discrimination. In fact, all castes did it in some fashion or another. The lower castes had castes beneath them, and even they would, strangely enough, practice discrimination.

I am going to take a short detour before I resume my narrative.

India became independent in 1947, and around 1950, Kerala had elected its first leftist government—indeed, the first ever democratically elected leftist government anywhere in the world. The reformation movement started by Mannath Padmanabhan and the general philosophy of equality among all the people, as espoused by the leftist manifesto, began to crack the walls of bigotry that had been, in my opinion, a blot on Hindu society.

In the early fifties in India, during my stint as a teacher and later as an employee of the Federal Audit Service, my circle of friends had widened considerably. I had close friends from all castes, including a few from those called—shamefully I might add—"untouchables".

And I was glad to notice during my erratic and infrequent visits to India from overseas that the strictures were being eased slowly through the years. Having said this, I also note with sadness that, today, there are still pockets of resistance to reformation here and there in the state.

Continuing the narrative.

Developments in the colonies that had already become independent in the wake of the British withdrawal from India made news back home because the indigenous population was gradually expressing their displeasure at Indians, who were holding high positions in the civil service, who owned huge estates, and who were in control of the economy. Many people of Indian origin left Sri Lanka, Myanmar, Singapore, and Malaysia before facing discrimination from the native population.

So, perhaps, it was not very surprising for me to discover that, in Uganda, discrimination among people of different communities—indigenous and expatriates—was alive and well. Uganda has many tribal communities and, at one time, had three kingdoms, each with its own king. Each kingdom had many tribes, and the inter-tribal affinity was almost non-existent to say the least. Uganda was home to many Asians, and the relationship between them and the Africans was also somewhat tenuous. But everyone appeared to be *united* under the British rule. What happened after the country became independent—the brutal regime of Amin, the expulsion of expatriates and such—is a matter of history.

But another curious matter came to light also. The ruling class practiced racial and class distinctions rather openly too!

The non-whites were not allowed to play golf! Period. But even among the whites, there was a class distinction. For instance, Kampala, the capital, had two "European" clubs—The Kampala Club and The Kampala Sports Club. The former was restricted to the upper strata of Britishers that included heads of departments, permanent secretaries (much like Deputy Ministers in Canada), higher officers of the army, police, banks etc. It was a very elite club. All other Britishers were members of the latter. This club admitted Europeans, as well, who could not get membership in the elite club, unless they belonged to the Diplomatic Corps. I personally know this because a good friend, Chris, a full-blooded Anglo Saxon, one of the members of the staff of the school in Kampala where I was teaching, could not gain membership in Kampala Club! He was a good tennis player, and Kampala Club had its own private courts, and Kampala Sports Club did not. He had to settle for the next best thing—playing on municipal courts with colored people. I recall entering the Uganda championships in tennis, and the matches were played at the Kampala Club; but we could not use the washrooms in the building! They had arranged temporary potties in the vast, well-manicured yard around the club for the duration of the tournament.

I am talking of the nineteen fifties! One would think that the passage of time, impact of globalization, migration of cultures, etc., would dampen the fervor with which the discrimination card was played. Consider what columnist Nick Cohen of the London newspaper *The Observer* wrote after the Tories and the Liberal Democrats formed a coalition in June 2010 to run the British government.

> *The sight of Nick Clegg and David Cameron joshing in the grounds of Downing Street had rammed home the truth about Britain that all the talk of "inclusion" and "diversity" obscures. We live in the most class-ridden society in Western Europe, and it is becoming more sclerotic and more hierarchical by the year. Look hard at a picture of our new government, and you could be forgiven for thinking that the 20th century never happened.*

I don't want to belabor the point, but we know that distinctions based on race or caste or class or ethnic origin have, across the world, wreaked havoc (and are continuing to do so)—be it in India, Africa, South East Asia, Eastern Europe, the Middle East, the Americas, or wherever.

But while growing up, the practice had not personally impacted me very much (except that it bothered me mentally) until the subcontinent was partitioned. The decision to divide India, when it was done, has to go down in history as one of the most serious blunders ever committed by a governing power. The event took place without adequately preparing the country for a seismic change. Lord Mountbatten wanted to retire in glory, and he gave independence to the two countries *before* the actual partition. It suddenly became a religious issue. Partition itself happened without anyone actually being in charge. Hindus and Muslims who had been neighbors for several decades turned against one another. Millions on both sides were butchered. The rancor and ill will created at that time still remain, and indications are that they will only exacerbate.

But during partition, something very curious happened in my hometown, several hundred miles away from where the blood was flowing. We had many Muslims in the city, and all of a sudden, they felt victimized. One friend I grew up with was a Muslim. His name was Salim. Even though he had not been invited into our house, we had played together since we were six or so. We went to school together, sang together at concerts. But soon after partition, he decided not to have any relationship whatever with me. Left to himself, he would not have ever *considered* doing anything like that. His parents pressured him. It was the typical reaction of a Muslim who felt that the Hindus were responsible for the partition and the resultant bloodshed. I was quite devastated.

I was just nineteen!

But a day in early March 1955 has been indelibly imprinted in my memory. My family and friends had gathered at the railway station to bid me good-bye and send me off to Mumbai, *en route* to Uganda. Just a few minutes before the train was due to leave, I noticed a familiar figure lurking in the corner of Higginbothams, the ubiquitous book stall one found on the platform of every major railway station in India. It was Salim. I rushed to him, and we stood in a tight embrace. We said nothing. We just looked at each other. Our tears told the whole story. Many years later, I would read that he died of cancer.

Perhaps for the first time, I felt ashamed of myself and the system that permitted the practice of such bigotry. But, as I had already mentioned, I was to find out soon that the malady was widespread, and as I write this, there are only feeble signs of abatement.

In Uganda, I was assigned to teach in a higher secondary school in Kololo, a suburb of Kampala, the capital. The majority of students were Asians. There were a few Ugandans and Brits, as well. The staff consisted of Asians and a few Europeans, but no Ugandans. But if one listened to the discourse and small talk in the faculty lounge, one could read the subtext of mild hatred in dropped statements. Sometimes it would surface like, "these Gujaratis, these Sardarjis, these Bengalis," etc. Yet they were all unanimous in their hatred of the British!

I recalled how, in India, the north generally disliked the south and vice versa; and in the south, the Keralites disliked the Tamils, the Tamils disliked the Andhraites, and so on. Nationally, the Punjabis disliked the Maharashtrians, the Maharashtrians disliked the Bengalis, and the Bengalis disliked everybody else! However if, for instance, a north Indian soccer team was playing a team from south India in one of the southern cities, regardless of which southern state the team came from, the crowd would howl the north Indians off the field!

I had occasion to experience this firsthand one time when I was in Singapore. I was *en route* to Bali where I was doing research for my post-graduate work on rituals and masks. The Indian soccer team was playing an exhibition match with the Singaporeans. I believe the Indians were on their way to compete in the Asian Olympics in Manila. Singapore has many Indians, many of them belonging to the second and third generation. Singapore was their motherland. And yet, during the game, the Indians in the crowd lustily cheered the visiting side, resulting in a stern rebuke from the then Prime Minister Lee Kuan Yew the next day. He said that he was disgusted at the behavior of the crowd, and if they were partial to the Indian team, they should go back to where they came from.

A few weeks after I started writing this, the state of Arizona passed a bill that would enable the law enforcement agencies to stop and query any person who is suspected to be an illegal Mexican immigrant. During an interview, the Governor was asked how she would *actually* identify an illegal immigrant. She was momentarily stumped, and then she simply said that she did not know. But she ought at least to know that many East Asians look like Mexicans. In fact, President Calderón looks very much like one of the Chemistry professors I had when I went to college.

Many native Indians look like Mexicans. Can a Keralite look like a Turkish Cypriot?

The answer would be "yes".

In the summer of 1970, the University of Athens, in collaboration with the University of London, had organized a two-week seminar in Greek theatre. Since I was an alumnus of the University of London, I was entitled to free tuition; but I had to take care of boarding and lodging.

I was contemplating a visit to India anyway. It was summer, my second child was too young to travel, and so I decided to go on my own, leaving the family behind in Boyle, Alberta, where I was the Principal of the high school.

The format of the course was the following: we would do an in-depth study of a Greek play for two days and, in the evening of the second day, we would see an actual production of it, followed the next day by a discussion of the production, and so on.

I checked into a moderately priced hotel in Athens. I used to walk to the university campus and, on the third day, I noticed that a flashy Mercedes Benz convertible was parked in an alley beside the hotel. I noticed it only because I am an automobile buff and felt sort of violated that someone would even think of parking such a magnificent automobile in a very dirty street!

As it happened, I saw the car every day, and I dismissed it as nothing too important; perhaps it belonged to the manager, I told myself.

It turned out to be beastly hot that summer, temperatures rising to 120° Fahrenheit during the day. Early in the second week, I decided that I'd had enough of it. Though I was born and raised in the humid tropics, the heat in Athens was unbearable, and so I decided to cut short my stay and go to India.

The flight out of Athens was around 3:00 p.m. as I recall; but I thought that there was no point in waiting until checkout time in the drab foyer of the hotel. So I called a cab and proceeded to the airport. When the taxi was going around one of the many traffic circles in the city, I thought I saw the same Mercedes Benz following us. When I reached the airport, obviously I went to the counter for an early check-in. At the counter, the clerk asked me for my passport—something that was not done those days. You showed the passport only at the immigration counter. When I asked about this deviation from usual practices, the lady smiled and politely said that she would like to see the document. I acceded, and after a couple of minutes or so, a uniformed man came and asked me to follow him. I did and was taken to a closet-sized room with a small table and two chairs. The man closed the door.

I sat there for what I thought was an eternity. To say that I was petrified would be a gross understatement. I wondered what I could possibly have done to provoke something like this. After a while, another man, who appeared to be a top brass in the armed forces, walked in with a grim face and sat down opposite me. For a few seconds all he did was just look at me! Then, he deliberately opened a file while still looking at me. No smile on that face, I noticed.

Then the interrogation began. My name, place of birth, what I was doing in Greece, what my occupation was, why I went to Uganda, why I moved to Canada, and so on and so forth. At one point, when I said that I was born and raised in India, he said, "You don't speak like an Indian." I was ready with a quick retort to ask him to tell me how, indeed, Indians spoke. But commonsense prevailed and I just kept quiet. I also noticed that he was repeating the questions at random, possibly in an attempt to trip me. I was obviously frightened but, at one point, I interrupted him and asked him what the fuss was all about. He simply said that it was best just to answer the questions and not ask any.

As if I had any choice!

I told him that I had answered all the questions truthfully. I believe the interrogation lasted for approximately twenty minutes. Then he left.

About ten minutes later, another man walked in. This time, it happened to be a civilian. He had a broad smile and was trying to convey the message that he was there to help and advised me that it was to my benefit if I gave only true answers to the questions. I repeated that I had given only honest and true answers. He just smiled. He had the same file and asked the same questions. I had the same answers, of course. I also had the same question—what it was about—and the answer was the same.

After questioning me, he left, and about ten minutes later, the first guy came back. He said that it appeared that I had two identifying marks on the body—one, pock marks on the face and the other, a mole on the third finger of the right hand.

Now, this might sound strange to some of you. In the fifties and sixties, those who applied for a passport had to provide this information, viz. permanent identifying marks on the body. They were listed on page two of the passport under the heading "Special Peculiarities"!

The officer proceeded to examine my finger and started to rub the mole off with some foul smelling fluid. My feeble protests that his experiment was hurting me were ignored. Then he mumbled something like, "It is genuine all right," and left the room.

After a while, he came back to say that I was free to go. Well, not so fast, I told myself. I politely asked him why I had been detained and questioned. The response was startling! Three weeks before, two Turkish Cypriot terrorists had killed a Greek industrialist; they were carrying Canadian passports, and one of them looked like me!

So, how did they confirm that I was not *the* Cypriot? He did not answer.

"How about my luggage?" I asked.

"It has all been taken care of," he replied.

By now, I was emotionally wrung out. I was terrified during the whole time I was in the interrogation room. I was not at all looking forward to spending the rest of my life in a Greek jail, infested with rats and cockroaches and God knows what else! The very idea gave me the shivers. I needed something to restore my frayed nerves, and so I went to the bar in the departure lounge and ordered a stiff drink.

Just then, a handsome, youngish man wandered in and stood beside me and said that the drink was on him. He gave me my luggage tags and explained that he was with the Greek intelligence service and that he drove a Benz convertible. With that, he gave me a wink, apologized for any inconvenience caused, wished me good luck, and hurried away. Obviously, he had been following me around during my stay in Athens.

Today, when I am about to turn eighty-three, I look back in anger. Angry because I had to practice bigotry when growing up, had to experience bigotry as an adult—sometimes subtle, sometimes not so subtle, as in an advertisement that appeared in the *Evening Standard*, London, where, as students, my wife and I were looking for an apartment. It blatantly and boldly said, "Indians and dogs not allowed". This was in 1960.

Canada ostensibly prides itself on the "mosaic" that defines the population, and yet, it would be naïve to say that racism and bigotry do not exist in this country. As in the faculty lounge in Kololo, one does hear statements like "these Jamaicans, these Jews, these Chinese, these Filipinos," etc. One hears occasional cries for the immigrants to assimilate with the population of the adopted country and, yet, there is no clear definition of what this assimilation means. If it means that a woman from Saudi Arabia or Somalia should wear Western swimsuits when at the beach, it would be ludicrous. I tried to assimilate as much as I could, while I was in Uganda for ten years. I spoke fluent Swahili (I still can manage a fluent, if mistake-ridden, conversation in Swahili.) I had many Ugandan friends and had more than scant knowledge of the culture of Bagandans, Jaluos, Acholis, Langos, and other tribes. I had the privilege of attending secret rituals and ceremonies of some of the communities.

When I first landed in Kampala, I fell in love with the country. "The Pearl of Africa", as Winston Churchill called it, was to be my home. I wanted to live and die there. But, alas, it was not to be. Anti-Asian sentiments were only latent during the British rule. They surfaced with alarming fury when the British left.

That was when my wife and I decided to leave with our son, who had just turned one.

Thus in 1965, we immigrated to Canada. The county of Athabasca, Alberta, hired me to teach English in the high school in a small village called Boyle—population, 550!

In 1966 I was made the Principal.

CHAPTER TWO

UGANDA---THE PEARL OF AFRICA; AT LEAST IT USED TO BE!

From Kerala to Uganda was a great change. It would require another book to describe the country, its national parks, the ethnic diversity, the curious amalgam of social mores, the cultural differences between the various tribes, the role of expatriates in developing the country, and such. This book is a memoir and, hence, I will restrict myself to what happened to me personally, how the country or my stay in the country impacted me and my family, and perhaps mention my own contribution, albeit small, to the development of the country.

I am also going to describe how my tenure with the Education Department of the British Colonial Service personally benefited me immensely. Among other things, I got an incredible boost to my self-confidence and got the opportunity to meet my future wife. I was awarded a bursary to study in England for my post-graduate degree. I got to tour extensively in England and Europe. I also got the opportunity to drive around some of the greatest national parks and wild game reserves in Uganda, Kenya, and Tanzania. I climbed Kilimanjaro, and I had the privilege of meeting His Highness the Aga Khan.

In 1954, the British government had hired me, along with approximately sixty other people from all parts of India, to teach in the schools in Uganda. As I had mentioned, I was posted to the Higher Secondary School (HSS) in Kololo, a suburb of Kampala. HSS roughly corresponds to a junior college in Canada. The students took the first two years of university at the school. Students and teachers of Kololo called themselves Kololians.

There were many bachelors on staff, and we were all accommodated in a large house on Mackinnon Road. We had domestic staff for cooking, laundry, general cleaning, gardening, etc. The unmarried women teachers on the staff also were housed in a similar facility in another part of town. It was but natural that the bachelors gravitated toward Baskerville Avenue, where the women lived.

It is only fair to say that the men in the hostel were generally reckless. Suddenly, we had a lot of money to spend, to live a good life. We became owners of motorcycles, and we roamed around Kampala and the environs on those fearsome contraptions.

I also fell in love with the most beautiful woman I have ever met—Nalini Oza.

One day, one of the more adventurous members of the gang suggested that we should, during the summer break, tour the national parks on motorbikes. An older member of the staff, overhearing the conversation, cautioned that if we were going to be rash enough to try something insane like driving around the parks, which had no roads to speak of—only tracks—we should also arrange for a car to follow us, just in case something unexpected happened. Rhinoceros, elephants, and wild buffaloes could be unpredictable, he concluded.

So we enlisted the services of a reluctant faculty member, and he agreed to follow us around in his car.

And so we set out.

The first day was uneventful. For the first time in our lives, we saw thousands of wild animals in their natural habitat. The second day, early in the afternoon, we were negotiating a winding, treacherously uneven track when we saw ahead of us a clump of trees. When we turned at a U bend, we also saw a herd of elephants of varying ages right in the middle of the track and under the trees. There were over a dozen animals, approximately forty feet away. We panicked and got off the bikes and crowded ourselves in the car. One of the bikes, a big Norton 750 (those days that was the most powerful motorbike available) lost its balance and fell sideways. Also, the owner had forgotten to turn off the engine, and so it was making puffing sounds.

For what appeared to be an eternity, everything was deathly quiet: the animals out in the open and the humans in the car cowed down with fear. Then grandpa decided to investigate the noise produced by the thing lying on the ground. Unfortunately, it touched the hot exhaust with its trunk and belted out a loud bellow, the likes of which I have never heard in my life! The angry animal then lifted the machine with its trunk and flung it wherever it might go. Before our very eyes, we saw the motorbike crash into a tree and a severely mangled machine hanging from the branches. We were sure that the car would be the next target. But after the exhibition of strength and fury, the herd left. We returned *sans* one very expensive motorbike. The sage in the faculty lounge would later say that we ought to consider ourselves very lucky that the elephants chose not to vent their anger at the car, which was a larger target.

Wild living continued. Courting Nalini continued. Occasionally, she would ride on the pillion of my bike. Meanwhile I had been having my share of accidents on the bike, as well, mostly due to speeding, exhibitionism, and in some cases, inclement weather. After the twelfth accident, which required several stitches above my right eyebrow (the scar is still there as a stark reminder of those wild days), Nalini gave me an ultimatum. I had to make a choice: the motorbike or her. Obviously, I sold the bike and invested in a Volkswagen beetle.

I believe I established a reputation as a good teacher of English. I recall that once the Headmaster wandered into the class unannounced. This was within a few months of my arrival in Kololo. He sat at the back of the classroom for about ten minutes and then left. I was sure I'd made a hash of things! I was certainly nervous. He could fire me that very day if he so chose or get me transferred to another school. Strangely enough, he did not mention anything about his visit that day or any other time. I argued that if I were no good, I would have known about it in a hurry.

During the third year in Kololo, I was promoted to the position of Senior Master of English. This was a landmark event, because I became the first non-native speaker to head the English department in the whole system. There were many native speakers of English on staff at Kololo and elsewhere, and they were, to say the least, chagrined. One of them even refused to talk to me! But many of them were wives of civil servants in other government departments, and the Ministry of Education assumed that, because they were native speakers of English, they could teach the language.

This is a mistaken notion. I had the advantage of studying the language as a subject, much like chemistry or geography. I had better than average skills in spoken and written English, mostly because I had British teachers. The curriculum was very rigorous. We had to study the major authors. A great deal of attention was paid to style and speech.

But, most importantly, I believe, my easy facility to use the language and acquire fluency in it were in large part due to the strict rules at home. Reading was mandatory. My father and mother were avid readers. Malayalam, my mother tongue, has a very rich literature, but both my parents were fond of reading books in English.

My father also had the habit of writing well composed sentences in a big ledger, examples of exciting metaphorical usage, scintillating prose, and colorful, poetic pieces that he came across while reading whatever books he brought from the library. And I had to read them all and even memorize some of them! For this effort, occasionally, I got the ultimate reward: one eighth of a rupee (two annas, for those who remember!) to go to a movie. I cannot even begin to convert two annas into Canadian currency; it would, today, be worth a dime. Maybe. That fabulous amount gave us a seat on the floor in front of the screen, whereas the more affluent denizens lounged on rickety chairs behind us.

Anyway, going back to my teaching abilities, I must have been a cut above the rest, I suppose; otherwise, I can't imagine the Ministry appointing me to head the English department. But with the promotion also came a transfer to a town called Mbale in northern Uganda. They also had a Higher Secondary School. The following year, I was moved even further north to a town called Soroti. This was in 1959. While I was being kicked from pillar to post, Nalini continued to teach at Kololo. Though distance separated us, that year we decided to get married.

❦

Nalini, who hailed from Mumbai, is a Gujarati and belongs to a different caste and race (she is an Aryan and I am a Dravidian). She is a Brahmin and I am not. I am a Nair, only a half Brahmin, if I borrowed a bit of my father's pedigree. My grandfather was a Namboothiri, a cut above the Brahmins.[2] (More on Namboothiris appear in the chapter 'Helping Hands'.)

Whatever the social ranking, if we were back in India, an alliance between us might have been inconceivable. I suspect there would have been vociferous expressions of protest from both sides, certainly from my side.

Typically, a Gujarati wedding takes a long time—sometimes the whole day—whereas the Nair wedding lasts about fifteen minutes. We picked what we considered were the most important elements from the rituals of both cultures and orchestrated a thirty-minute function. We got surrogate parents. It should be mentioned, however, that early in 1959, we both were on home leave in India and had the opportunity of meeting our respective parents. But we announced our intention of getting married only after returning to

---

2   Namboothiris are considered the most orthodox Brahmins in India. They regard themselves as the true repositories of the ancient Vedic religion and of the traditional Hindu Code. The Namboothiri caste followed a distinctive alliance with the Nairs. The eldest son customarily married a Namboothiri woman; the younger sons were allowed to marry Nair women. Perhaps the most famous Namboothiri was Adi Shakaracharya, a philosopher who lived in the 9th century.

Uganda. Neither side expressed any objection and graciously gave their blessings. Later, we would be accepted in both families with love and understanding.

In 1960, I was posted back to Kololo from Soroti and, at the end of the year, I was awarded a bursary to study in London. I enrolled at the University of London, Institute of Education for post-graduate work in English, specializing in teaching English as a Foreign Language.

Nalini did not get a bursary because she was a married woman! In fact, soon after marriage, she lost all her perks, including pension. Chalk it up to one of the clauses in the British Civil Service Code! But she decided to accompany me and, to do this, she had to resign from her position at the school. She was thus without any salary for a year. But she went to teach in a school in Chelmsford in the east coast of England and took evening and weekend courses in London. She specialized in Reading.

From June 1960 through the following full year we were in England.

It was not possible to get suitable accommodation in London. So we went to Ilford in Essex. It was an easy half-hour commute either way—to London for me and to Chelmsford for Nalini.

When I got the details of my program of studies at the University of London, I noticed that many courses that I was mandated to attend were those that I had more than scant knowledge in. The Shakespeare courses were something I could romp through very easily. I had been teaching some of the plays for years. History of the English language was also something I was very comfortable with. I had read all the major poets. If only I could get exemption from attending a few courses, I could try to get instruction in another field, which was actually one of my passions—theatre. We already had the opportunity to see some of the giants of theatre on stage—Peter O'Toole and Richard Burton to name two. The productions had a great impact on me. They reignited dormant desires, and I desperately wanted to get instruction in and some exposure to the art and craft of directing.

This really meant getting permission to skip classes. So I gingerly went to two or three professors and explained the situation. Needless to say, this was a strange request! I assured them that I was not going to waste time but that I wanted to study other courses outside the college. The professors reluctantly agreed, as long as I wrote the final examinations. But I needed to get permission from the Head of the Department, Dr. Bruce Pattison.

"What courses and where?" thundered the professor.

When I mentioned that I would like to attend some of the courses at the Royal Academy of Dramatic Art, it appeared that he mellowed a bit. Later on, I would discover that he was a theatre buff himself. He sternly reminded me that RADA did not take drop-in students, they screened students assiduously and admitted only those who wanted to pursue a career in professional theatre. I said that I was quite aware of it. I explained that I had permission to attend some of the courses as an observer. But I was reminded—again—that I had to write the final exams in *all* courses if I had any hopes of getting a degree. I said that I realized that only too well. I was enrolled in eight courses and I had to write exams in all of them during the exam week. If I failed in one, I would fail to get a degree. The system did not allow a student to write repeat exams in just the failed courses.

At RADA, I was a novelty. For starters, I was the only Indian student. There were two West Indians, but they were second-generation Brits. The school was not, as mentioned before, used to accommodating observers. The few courses that I had the privilege of sitting in were very rewarding. But the most invaluable experience was an evening course offered by a man called Martin Esslin.

I am sure that Esslin is not known beyond the circle of those who are active practitioners of theatre. He was teaching a course called, I believe, "Modern Theatre". I had no idea that I was going to witness the birth of a concept that would revolutionize dramaturgical thinking forever—Theatre of the Absurd.[3]

---

3   Theatre of the Absurd is not a movement. It is a designation for particular plays that fall under this category—plays which had a pessimistic vision of humanity struggling vainly to find purpose in life and control its fate. This came about as a result of World War Two. It took the basis of existential philosophy and combined it with dramatic elements to create a style of theatre, which presented the world as something that could not be logically explained.

Esslin *created* the term. I am thrilled to say that I was *there* when he said something like, "I want to call it *The Theatre of the Absurd.*" A large number of students cramped into the small classroom—many of them squatting on the floor, right up to the podium. We listened with rapt attention to the Hungarian immigrant who looked and dressed like a diplomat. His lecture notes would eventually be published as "Experimental Theatre". It is considered a seminal work in the field.

As I had mentioned before, I was specializing in the teaching of 'English as a Foreign Language' in London. This entailed practicum in countries where English is considered a foreign language.

Many of my colleagues were sent to Spain; but a few, including me, were sent, of all places, to North Wales! Though the people there spoke Welsh, I could not understand why they would be considered foreign speakers of English.

In any event, I did not complain. Ever since I had read *How Green Was My Valley* when I was young, I had dreamt of wandering around Welsh mining towns. I was sent to teach two weeks each in two schools—one in Portmadoc and another in Caernarvon. In addition to teaching the Welsh students a "foreign" language, I experienced two very curious incidents! Both were amusing as well.

The first happened when I was in Portmadoc. One day, Pritchard-Jones, one of the teachers, invited me for supper. He had told his two sons—eight and ten—that an Indian would join them for meals that evening. I went with my host immediately after classes. When we reached the house, two boys greeted us, dressed as Aboriginal Indians—body paint, feathers, tomahawk, the whole works! What was embarrassing for Pritchard-Jones was that even his wife appeared to have misunderstood that the guest was going to be a "Red Indian"! She actually helped the kids to get their faces painted and get into the fancy costumes—all in my honor!

Another incident happened when I was in Caernarvon. One morning when I walked into the staff room, I found the teachers in a state of wild aggravation. A few teachers were talking in Welsh and others in English. I caught one sentence, "I don't think we bloody well should" or something strong like that. I asked what the commotion was about, and one of the sober ladies told me that the school had been "ordered" to let the primary classes off for the morning, so that they could stand along the main thoroughfare in the town, wave flags, and welcome Princess Margaret, who was on an official visit to the castle! I had no idea that the Welsh—some of them at any rate—harbored such anti-monarchist feelings.

Though many interesting and exciting things happened to us during our stay in England, one experience stands out. One day we received a letter from the Lord Chamberlain of Buckingham Palace. The astonishment was further enhanced by the fact that it was addressed to my wife! When we opened it, we realized that it was an invitation, indeed a command, to tea at the Palace. We were both members of the Commonwealth Students Union; but I was very chagrined that only my wife would get invited and not me as well! But that was transitory. We looked forward to the event. We learned later that the invitations went to about one hundred commonwealth students. The Queen and Prince Philip greeted Nalini. They exchanged pleasantries. The queen particularly commented on the sari that Nalini was wearing. (The participants were asked to wear their national dress.)

All in all, with London as the base, we traveled widely in the British Isles and Europe. I believe we managed to visit twenty-one countries in Europe—even camping for the first time in our lives!

On our return to Uganda in 1961, we noticed that that the mood of the country had changed dramatically. *Africanization* was the mantra. At the dawn of freedom in 1962, Mr. Milton Obote, the Prime Minister, had publicly guaranteed that the expatriates would be "safe" under the new regime. But that was to change. And I also noticed something very strange and amusing. Before independence, I was not white enough to become a senior administrator, say a Headmaster or an Inspector of Schools. I had to be satisfied with the position of Senior Master. But now, I realized that I was not black enough!

In reference to this, I have to flash back a bit and describe something that happened while I was in Mbale in 1958. There, in the tennis club, I met a man called Henry Barlow. He was very much interested in English literature as I was and so we really connected. In fact he wrote a lot of poetry, as I recall. He used to lament the fact that even though he had a degree from London or Oxford (I am not very sure) he had to be satisfied with being a clerk in the department of agriculture. His boss was much less qualified, but he was white and that was all that mattered.

Henry used to dream of the day when the country would be independent, how there was bound to be an agricultural revolution, and how he would play a very important part in that revolution, how he would help improve the life of the typical farmer, and so on. When he waxed eloquent, he was sincere, patriotic, and a tad dreamy.

On my return from London, I was posted back to Kololo. On the first day of school, I did what I always do—check the class list and give faces to the names. I noticed one Dennis Barlow on the list. Of course, I had to ask him if he was any relation of Henry. Yes, they were brothers. He wanted to do his two years at Kololo and go to London to get his degree in education. He hoped that he would have the privilege of joining the faculty at Kololo.

I told him that I did not see any reason why he couldn't.

Immediately after independence, many Englishmen in senior administrative positions voluntarily retired. Qualified Ugandans were replacing them. It was no surprise, therefore, that Henry Barlow got a plum job. He became the Permanent Secretary in the Ministry of Agriculture. That was the highest non-political job one could aspire to get in the government, except the position of Chief Secretary.

I must say that I had lost contact with him when I left Mbale. But when I read in the newspaper that Henry had been appointed to head the department, I sent him a letter of congratulations. He did not respond. I assumed that he did not recollect who I was.

But, as I said earlier, the fever of *Africanization* was gripping the country. The clamor for making the dream a reality was getting louder.

It was clear that we had no future in that country. The British government advised the expatriates to leave as soon as possible. If we did early enough, we would be guaranteed a pension for life, eligible for the number of years served.

So in 1964, we filed the papers.

One day, I got a call from Henry, asking if I would kindly meet him. I agreed and, during our meeting, he told me that he had gathered from the Establishment Department that I had filed papers for retirement. He also said that the Prime Minister had asked all heads of departments to talk to those who were trying to leave and encourage them to stay on.

"The country cannot afford to let go people like you," Henry said.

I said that it was very flattering, but could he guarantee that we would be able to hold our positions? "For instance, when your brother Dennis returns from London with a teaching degree, suppose he and I both applied for the Headmaster's job, who is likely to get it?" I said.

He mumbled something and went on the defensive.

We left in 1965 before Idi Amin took over. It is a matter of record that Amin murdered hundreds of the intelligentsia, including civil servants in the upper echelons and thousands of soldiers and farmers who did not belong to his tribe. The Minister of Health, Dr. Henry Kyembe, was spared and allowed to live, if he would sign death certificates declaring that the victims died of natural causes. For fear of his life and that of his family, he acquiesced. But he was secretly plotting to leave the country. First, he sent the family away to London. He followed them later and sought political asylum in England. In return, he disclosed all that he knew. Further, he documented the atrocities in a book called *A State of Blood.* This book, published in 1977, has an appendix, which lists the names of the people in high office who had been murdered.

In 1954, when I was getting ready to leave India for Uganda, I was told that there was a student from Uganda, attending the university. His name was Joseph Mubiru. He was on a scholarship from the government of India.

I made it a point to meet him to get firsthand information about the country. We often met for coffee or lunch. I also got my first lessons in Swahili! He came to see me off when I left for Uganda.

But I had lost touch with him over the years. It appears that Mubiru went to the London School of Economics and later became an officer in the World Bank. In 1961, Obote brought Mubiru to Kampala to take over as the Governor of the Central Bank.

Kayembe's list includes Mubiru.

I believe that Henry was jailed and whipped by Amin, but not killed. I have a vague recollection that he fled to Ethiopia or some other African country.

Before I bring closure to this chapter, I would like to mention two things I am rather proud of.

The first is that, on the eve of Uganda's independence, the British government awarded me a medal of honor for distinguished services to the crown. I was one of one thousand, and the recipients included Europeans, Asians, and Ugandans.

Second, while I was in Mbale, I had the privilege of meeting His Highness the Aga Khan, the spiritual leader of the Muslim sect known as Ismailis. East Africa had a large number of Ismailis and as such it was only natural that he visited the countries. His installation ceremonies were held at various locations over 1957 and 1958. Thus it was that he came to Mbale, which had a sizeable number of Ismailis. In Mbale, the senior administrators of the school were invited to be presented to him, and I was personally introduced to him. We shook hands and exchanged pleasantries. He was a very young man then, twenty one, I believe. He was dressed in white, as I recall—a very sophisticated person with a polite demeanor. The memories are very vivid.

I am about to bring closure to my account of our stay in Uganda. There are many more exciting stories to tell. But one experience that Nalini and I believe unforgettable is a night spent in the Treetops Hotel in Kenya. As the name suggests, the hotel is built on the branches of a tree. Literally. For instance, in our bedroom there was a thick branch through the wall and over the bed, and out again! Obviously you kept the lights on all the time, unless you wanted a huge bump on your forehead when getting up! The clients checked in late in the afternoon and, from the balcony we watched wild animals that came to the waterhole and salt-lick approximately fifty feet away. We could go to bed whenever we wanted, but we could also request the guards to wake us up if a large herd of rhinos or elephants arrived to get a drink or lick the salt. The hotel is probably best remembered as the place where Princess Elizabeth came to know of the death of her father King George VI. This was in 1952, but Mau Mau terrorists burned down that particular structure. In two years, the government built a new and larger hotel on another tree close by.

Apart from the safaris, climbing Kilimanjaro, marriage, studying abroad, and such, the stint in Uganda turned out to be very important in another way. Earlier, I had made a passing reference to my self-confidence. I was hopelessly lacking it over the years leading up to the departure for Africa, especially in the academic field. To the chagrin of my parents, I turned out to be a very mediocre student, during my school days, and even during my first four years at the University. Except in English and in Natural Science, my performance at the academic level was nothing spectacular. I just managed to get passing grades. But as a graduate student in London, I managed to ace the examinations and passed with distinction, as the diploma testifies. I would do the same thing later. I passed my M.Ed. from the University of Montana with a grade point average of 4.0,[4] and in my MFA from New York University, I got "A pluses" in all courses.

I had often wondered about this. I am not a psychologist and, as such, I have not done any self-analysis. I admit that I don't have an explanation. When I was growing up, did anything scar my sensibilities so badly as to prevent applying myself to acquire educa-

---

4   Grade Point Average: A quantitative measure of an academic record on a scale of 1.0 to 4.0

tional excellence, which is a pre-requisite for any advancement in life? I suppose I could find something or someone to blame, but I believe it would be counter productive and would sound alarmingly self-defensive! But I do think that, when you are six or seven, it is difficult to comprehend the differences in social status and the resultant discrimination based on abstractions like caste.[5] So did the blatant bigotry that I was exposed to affect my sensibilities somehow? I don't know.

Anyway, it is perhaps correct to say that I grew up without any interest in academic pursuits and without a sense of what I wanted to do with my life. I did what my parents asked me to do. The only three activities that I really enjoyed were reading, tennis, and theatre.

Maybe this is a good time to go back in history and give an account of my childhood and my growing years. But, before I embark on that part of my life, let me say that I am reminded of an aphorism by Graham Greene—*there is always a moment in childhood*

5   On the 15th of August 2010, India celebrated its 64th anniversary. Many decades ago, caste discrimination was banned in India. And yet, it was curious to read a news item published on August 13, 2010, by *Agence France-Presse*. It reported that just three days before the anniversary—when the country would be crowing about its freedom, economic power, and other "achievements", the government approved the inclusion of caste details for the first time in the ongoing census, to provide government with data for policies, aimed at helping deprived sections of society. A senior spokesperson for the government helpfully said, "Caste will be canvassed without affecting the integrity of the head count."
The rumbling you just heard is Mahatma Gandhi rolling in his grave!

when the door opens and lets the future in. That moment had escaped me, and the "future," from my childhood, up to the time I left India, somehow was behind closed doors, secured by heavy lock and key.

CHAPTER THREE

TWENTY-SEVEN YEARS OF MEDIOCRITY

As I have mentioned earlier, my father moved to the suburbs when I was three years old.

The enduring and endearing memory of the house in which I grew up is that there was a lot of color and fragrance about the place. In addition to a hundred or so rose bushes, we had plants and trees that produced sweet-smelling flowers, like jasmine. Some of them like the frangipani, golden champa (magnolia family), and madagandhi (devil's tree) blossomed at night and exuded a very strong fragrance. My parents used to sit outside, especially during moonlit evenings, and I have a vague recollection of cuddling beside them. But the overwhelming fragrance about the place is a vivid memory.

We also had many coconut palms, mango trees and banana plants. We had three jackfruit trees of which mention will be made later. In Kerala (I suspect in other states too), we have a habit of naming houses as well, and my father called our house "Sukumara Park". Obviously it was in honor of the number one son!

Many of my earlier memories are hazy, but I know that, for a while, I was the only child in the house, until my younger sister came along, when I was five or so.

My mother would, after sending my father away to work, do the household chores, take a bath and, after lunch, spend time reading books or doing embroidery, crochet, and such. We did not have a cook, but a "poor relation" used to come twice a week to dust and mop the house. We had "lower caste" neighbors who swept the yard, drew water from the well, cleaned the utensils, washed clothes and did other chores.

My mother had a habit of reading aloud to herself. In retrospect, I think that she was trying to ensure that I heard the sounds of English. And, I am told, I would wander about trying to repeat the words I had heard. Mother especially mentioned the word "thunderbolt". So, even before I went to school, I had this somewhat large, passive vocabulary, though I had no clue whatever of the meaning of the words. This must have developed my great love for the words in the language. Even today, many times, I ruminate on a particular word and the experience it creates within me. Sometimes, I don't get it. How in the world does one capture the essence of the words "exhilarating" or "exquisite"?

My love affair with the words in this beautiful language continues.

I remember that, when my father returned from work, my mother would narrate the story of the novel she had been reading.

She would continue where she left off the previous day. Father preferred biographies and the classics. No escape literature for him! I recall that, once, he tried to translate David Copperfield into Malayalam. But he abandoned the project because of a lack of time. Or perhaps he thought that it was not an easy thing to do. Whether a translation could or would capture the essence of the original had always been something that had intrigued me, especially after reading English translations of Russian and French writers. I recall that when, in 1972, I decided to direct *Hedda Gabler* by Ibsen, I had dearly wished to discuss the translation with a Norwegian drama-turge! Does the translation do justice to the original?

Anyway, coming back to my father's attempts, I am sure he realized that he was no expert on nineteenth-century England, and that he could not possibly bring to his effort either the dexterity of Dickens or the essential atmosphere of the setting. For that matter, he probably was not a scholar in Malayalam either. In any event, he had to take care of his dear garden. And do the crossword puzzles.

One of the books that captivated my mother was called *Vendetta*, by Marie Corelli. This particular detail I did not know when I was very young, of course, but I did, apparently, remember my mother telling my father about this man who was out to kill a woman, and she screamed, pleaded with him not to kill her, etc. Mother would tell me later that, after listening to the narrative, I would, in my solitary moments, impersonate the characters and perform a "scene". I am sure that I did not know, then, the connotation of the word "kill" or why anyone should kill another person, whatever the action meant. Apparently this man threw a huge rock on the woman, who was already in something called a "coffin". But I would go around reenacting the scene, as it were, muttering lines in Malayalam. Apparently, I spoke fluent Malayalam before I was three. Perhaps a thespian had been born.

I had an older sister who died when she was two or three years old and I was one. Her name was Shyamala. It appears that, in 1929, there was a serious epidemic of smallpox and many people died, mostly due to the unavailability of proper treatment.

Inevitably, I contracted the dreadful disease. In fact, many people in my family caught small pox—easy when you have a joint family system—though none were as serious as mine. Everyone in the family thought that I was going to die. My mother told me that it was a miracle that I survived. I was bed ridden for over a month. But beyond bedsores and such, I developed a peculiar condition. I was told that my head grew out of shape, and it looked like I was sprouting two horns! My grandfather had considerable influence in the medical department, and he pressed into service one of the specialist doctors who collaborated with an Ayurvedic physician. Together, they massaged my head back into shape. However, the top of the head would remain soft, until I was seven or so.

I believe I learned to read and write quite early because I know that I skipped the first two grades when I was admitted to the primary school. Obviously, I was younger than the rest of the class; and I was a diminutive kid and easy prey for the bullies. During recess, when we were allowed to play in the schoolyard, the top of my head would begin to pulsate, possibly because of the heat—much like the underside of the mouth of a frog at rest. So, obviously, I was nick-named the "frog". But one day, things got out of hand and a bully poked his pencil through my scalp. Since the skull was not yet fully formed, the pencil apparently went through the skin. I don't know if it hit the brain. Possibly. Or possibly not. In those days, the hospitals did not have the equipment to determine such things...certainly not in my hometown. But it did bring an angry father to the school to have a stern talk with the Headmaster. I must also say that I have no recollection of this incident.

I don't remember much, if anything, of my primary school days, except that I was very poor in arithmetic. I probably was suffering from what is known as "dyscalculia", a neurological disorder that makes it tough for children to learn arithmetic. So my father got me a private tutor, who actually was the same teacher who taught me the subject in the school. He would struggle to make me understand the intricacies of addition, multiplication, division, finding percentages, and such, but I somehow could not get a grip on what I thought were complicated procedures. The frustrated teacher would resort to corporal punishment by pinching me. The procedure hurt, of course, but I gritted my teeth and bore it. At the end of the lesson, my arm would be covered with bruises. Obviously, I had not told my parents that the teacher was brutalizing me! But one day, my mother noticed the bruises when I was taking a bath. I vividly recall my mother standing behind the door (modesty would not allow her to talk directly to a stranger, even though he was my tutor) asking the teacher why he was hurting me. She also said that if I did not master the essentials of arithmetic, so be it. No more punishments. I suppose the teacher felt very badly about it. Poor man, he was only trying to do what he thought was best. You know, spare the rod and spoil the child stuff!

Middle School was four years. Father was convinced that what I needed was discipline, and so he sent me to a Jesuit private school two miles away, instead of a public school half a mile away. It was also drilled into me that he was paying for my schooling (it was free in the public school system), and so I had better smarten up! I had to walk to the school, because there was no other way of getting there. There was no public transportation of any kind. In fact, I don't recall seeing city buses, until I was fourteen or so. Mother would pack my lunch in what were called "tiffin boxes" though they were not strictly boxes. They were neat little things: three round brass bowls stacked one on top of the other. Each bowl was approximately five inches in diameter and three inches deep. The bottom one contained rice, the middle one had some kind of curry, and the top had a vegetable dish. These three bowls were held in place by an intricate arrangement of a lid and a frame in the shape of a loop. A metal bar kept the loop in place. The bar had a flat end, and it served as a spoon as well.

There were nothing like vending machines in those days and, so, the only drink available was water. The school had no running water. So we had to draw water from a well.

On Saturdays, we had a music teacher come to our house to teach me Carnatic music. I believe that I had a gift for singing and that I had a pleasant singing voice. I suppose I still do, though, now, I would not dream of subjecting anyone to the pain of listening to my crooning! I wanted to continue training in the music academy, but it was about six miles away, and in any event, my father did not want me to stray away from the straightforward academic route. Given an option, though, I would have tried to become a professional musician.

Middle school was a drag, and I generally did poorly, though I excelled in English, natural sciences, and drawing. My so-called excellence in English also provided comic relief once in a while.

I recall one time I made an ass of myself, when my father and I went to the local military hospital. The administrator of the hospital was a distant relative. It appears that my father was not keeping well. Later, he would be diagnosed with severe bronchitis. He was a heavy smoker. Anyway, from the hospital dispensary, my father used to get every month a few boosters, tonics, and vitamins. One of them had the words "shake well" on top of the lid of a largish bottle, and I noticed it because it was written in stylish, cursive letters. The tonic was actually called Metatone, which I did not know.

During one of these visits, I recall my father suggesting to his friend that a particular tonic that he got a few months before was more efficacious than the others. So, the man asked for the name, but it had slipped my father's mind. And I shot up with the answer "shake well". The two men burst into laughter. Needless to say, I was humiliated. I did not know what was funny, either, until the man brought the bottle and showed me the label.

One thing I distinctly remember of my middle school years is an event called "meeting". Once in two weeks, during the last hour on Friday, the class held a meeting. The form teacher presided. It was a pretty formal affair, which began with a prayer song, followed by the minutes of the previous meeting. The job of keeping minutes was rotated, to enable as many students as possible to take on what was considered an important role. One student would make a speech or read a speech on a subject of the speaker's choice. There was also recitation of prose and poetry pieces. Sometimes, we read a fable or a short story. This would be in English or Malayalam.

In retrospect, I think it was an invaluable experience.

In the school, I met students of all castes, though the majority of kids were Christians. I made many friends, but I could not get them over on weekends to play in our very extensive yard. I especially wanted to invite a boy whose name was Anthony Henry. He lived in another part of the town. We played soccer together for the school. I still did not comprehend why there should be rules that would prohibit my friends to come and visit me. I only knew that I did not have the guts to confront my parents. Such things were just not done in a conservative Hindu household.

It was in the Middle School that I got the first opportunity to get on stage to sing and perform in plays.

One of the things I vividly recall is that, during the summer vacation in April and May, many of my cousins came to stay with us. They had limited space to play where they usually lived, and downtown was not interesting anyway. Both girls and boys came. It used to be quite a crowd, mostly from my father's side.

We had a lot of fun playing marbles, climbing trees, falling off trees, scraping our shin or elbows, playing on the swings, walking to the paddy fields about half a mile away, and splashing around in a creek that ran through the fields. Talking of bruises, when we got one, my mother would walk around the compound and bring the leaves of some medicinal herb, which she would grind into a paste with rice water and apply on the bruise. We did not have polysporin, Band-Aids, and such! A strip of cloth held the medicinal herb in place. In the evening, we slept on mats spread on the floor, because there were not enough cots and mattresses to go around.

The High School was in a different part of the city, but under the same management as that of the Middle School. We had excellent teachers, especially in English, but I barely made it through matriculation.

Something very traumatic happened to me during the first year of high school. It was sometime in July 1940. For some reason I am not sure of, my father suggested that I choose French as a second language, instead of Hindi. The teacher was a priest from some country in Europe. The French lessons were immediately after the noon hour recess. Every lesson started with a review of vocabulary taught during the previous lesson. The Jesuit schools firmly believed in not sparing the rod. The teachers were brutal in the use of the short dowels they carried, hidden in the wide sleeves of their loose-fitting cassocks.

Anyway, on this particular day, I decided to go to the class early and review the lesson. When I walked in, I saw the teacher with his head tilted back and putting something inside his nose, or at least I thought where his nose ought to be. When he saw me, he raised his head and looked at me. I let out a scream, because the man had no nose! I ran out of the class, with the teacher in pursuit, saying, "Don't be afraid, it is all right", or something to that effect.

I was shivering with fear, and I skipped classes and went home. The next day, my father got me enrolled in Hindi.

It appears that the man had a prosthetic nose, and he was trying to put some snuff into his nostrils, put the rubber nose back, and inhale.

This event had a serious impact on me psychologically, so that over the years, I found that learning French was not easy. There always was some kind of a mental block. I made many attempts to learn the language, especially when we had decided to move to Canada from Uganda. I attended a few classes offered by Alliance Francaise in Kampala, but I could not get ahead with it. Today, though, I can handle six or seven languages, but as far as French is concerned, I can understand only bits and pieces or get a vague idea of the essence of the dialogue.

∞

My already troubled mind would only be further aggravated by a tragic event in history: the Second World War.

I was eleven.

The first year of the war did not have much of an impact, as far as I remember, though the war was the most important news every day. I knew that things were getting to be scarce and expensive. The hope then was that the war would not last long.

Anyway, by the end of the second year, the government imposed rationing. Each family was issued a ration card, which entitled it to get a certain amount of rice, sugar, and kerosene every week.

Cooking oil was available for us in plenty because we used coconut oil for cooking, and we had plenty of coconuts in our compound. (By the way the word "Kerala" means the land of coconuts.) Cotton also had to be rationed, because it was required to make uniforms for soldiers, canvas for tents, backpacks, ropes, etc. But once every month, we could buy a certain length of cotton material as well.

It was my job to go to the ration shop every week to get the supplies. Mother had made a few sacks out of bed sheets and hired one of our neighbors to accompany me and carry the load. I usually carried the sugar, because that was the lightest load. The store, as I recall it, was about three miles away; but if I cut through paddy fields and used country lanes, the distance would be reduced by a mile. Every Saturday, I would trek to the store. It was to my advantage if I were not too far behind in the queue, and so, I would leave the house at the crack of dawn. Even so, there would be long line up. More than once when I had reached the front of the line, the shopkeeper would say that the week's supply of rice had been sold out, but I could have wheat or millet instead. In those days, the typical south Indian did not know what to do with wheat! We are basically rice eaters. Mother would get very angry at me for not arguing with the man and getting our ration that we were entitled to. Why wasn't I aggressive? Of course, there *was* enough rice, but the shopkeeper would keep it to sell in the black market. Black market prices were much higher, obviously, and sometimes we could not afford to buy all the rice we wanted. Mother, however, had a stock for special occasions like birthdays, festivals, and such. And my father's brother, who was a farmer approximately fifteen miles away from the city, would occasionally gift us a few bushels of paddy.

Rice was supplemented by jackfruit. The tree that bears this fruit is very large. (A picture of a jackfruit tree appears elsewhere in the book.) The fruit is the largest born by any tree in the world. Sometimes, the fruit weighs as much as eighty pounds. It has been recorded that some fruits grow as long as thirty-six inches in length and twenty inches in diameter! I must admit I have not seen anything that large. In our compound, at any rate, the fruits were as big as, perhaps, a beach ball. The exterior of the fruit looks like that of a durian—sort of. Inside the fruit is a plentiful supply of pulp, which, with the seeds, makes a good dish when cooked with spices—very much like a thickened version of jambalaya. We usually ate it with fish curry. (My father was a strict vegetarian, but my mother was not; and he did not mind non-vegetarian meals being cooked in the house.)

A typical jack tree produces over a dozen fruits at a time. The crop is available almost all the year round. The shortage of rice affected everyone, except those who owned paddy fields. So the poor people around our house would buy jackfruit, coconuts and, sometimes, mangoes from us. Mother steadily built a savings account from these sales. Sometimes, she would barter the fruits for sugar or kerosene. (Incidentally, what once was a deserted outskirt of the city when my father moved into in 1931 had now become a crowded little town called Kumarapuram.)

The price of vegetables also rose sharply because, across the state, many vegetable gardens were converted into cassava plantations. Cassava became the staple food of poor people. This meant that we had to grow our own vegetables and save money for other things. Father saved the rose bushes though, but other flowerbeds gave way to cucumber, okra, eggplant, beans, etc. Gone were the beautiful cannas, lilies, balsam, petunia, various kinds of sunflower, hollyhocks and, my favorite, nasturtium. I had a fascination with that plant with its round leaves and flowers with a tail. I was quite surprised to find that one could grow that plant here in Canada. I always try and grow a few nasturtiums in my garden.

I had a vague idea of why the war was being waged, but certainly no clear idea why India had to be part of the war. Also, I was very confused when I realized that the Nazi symbol was the swastika, which, in reality, is an ancient Hindu symbol. The hardships brought on by the war only aggravated the collective hatred toward the British.

I matriculated in 1943, but my marks were so low that the university refused me admission. My father pulled a few strings and got me in on the strength of my high marks in English.

The war ended in 1945, but India would wage a war of its own, viz. trying to get independence from the British. Gandhi's independence movement had become very strong. The students were strongly united behind it.

In the campuses, there were public meetings on a regular basis. Usually they would be to protest some anti-Indian law that had been passed by the British or the arrest of one of the political leaders. Those days, most public meetings started with a patriotic song. I was kind of a permanent fixture at the meetings in our campus. Compared with the student leaders, I was small, and, perhaps, I looked cute! I could certainly sing.

In 1948, I graduated with a degree in English and Botany. The results came out at the end of April, and what to do next was a burning question in the Nair household. A boost in income was called for to help my siblings through college. Thus it was that I became a teacher in a rural high school not very far from my home town. I was not sure if I was cut out to be a teacher, but once I got my feet wet, I realized that I did, indeed, like the profession. I also realized that, if I wanted to get ahead in the profession, I had to get a teaching degree, and hence, after two years of teaching I acquired one.

While I was a student in the Teachers Training College, I was also teaching English in a private college, which prepared students for matriculation, pre-degree, and degree examinations. Basically, it was a tutorial college. There I got valuable experience in teaching English.

A year after I graduated from the Training College, the Auditor General's office, which by now had become a federal affair, announced a nation-wide recruitment drive for training young, qualified people to join the officer's cadre. But they had to pass a rigorous written examination and an equally rigorous personal interview. By any standard, the job was much more lucrative than that of a teacher. As a teacher I got eighty rupees a month; as an auditor I would start at an astounding one hundred and twenty! I was also entitled to some twenty rupees or so as "Dearness Allowance", though I admit I don't know what the term means. Another distinct advantage was that, if I got the job, I would always be in my hometown, and I could stay with my parents; a teacher in the government system could be posted anywhere in the state. I also knew that my father would be thrilled.

Well, pragmatism won over idealism and prejudices. So, against my better judgment and brushing aside my antipathy toward numbers and a dislike for a sedentary job, I wrote the examination and appeared for an interview. I guess I did well, because I was selected as an officer in training. What saved my sanity was the part-time stint at teaching English in the private college. This I continued to do even though "moonlighting" was against federal policy. It was strange working in the same office with my father; but we never were in the same department.

One day, two years after auditing and exposing rogue departments and officers, I happened to see an advertisement in the paper inviting applications from qualified teachers to join the British Civil Service and teach in Uganda.

Without telling my parents, I sent in an application. Sometime late in October 1953, I believe, I got a letter from the British Protectorate asking me to appear for an interview. I was supposed to present myself at 2:00 p.m. at the Mascot Hotel, the only "star" hotel in Thiruvananthapuram at that time. I was told that two officers—Mr. W. B. Ouseley and Mr. K. D. Gupta—would be interviewing me.

After the initial shock ("*Why do you want to go to the Dark Continent when you have excellent career opportunities here?*"), my father told me that, if I were serious about the job, I should present myself for the interview in a suit, which, of course, I did not have. I did not even have a pair of pants! I usually wore a shirt and a dhoti (like a sarong), which was the ensemble that most Keralites wore every day, whatever the occasion. There were a few "Anglicized" locals who wore shirts and pants, but they were at that time a minority.

A suit means shoes as well. I had not seen many people in the city walking around with shoes on, except the Europeans, those in the army, or higher ranks in the police department. I, like most others, wore sandals. I was not about to buy a pair of shoes just for an interview, which I might fail!

Anyway, I collected the ensemble with great difficulty, I might add, thanks to contributions from several friends. There were no convenient buses to the location, and taxis were prohibitively expensive. So at around 12:30 p.m., resplendent in my borrowed clothes, I trekked down to the hotel. I would later think that if the owners of my "couture" demanded their contributions back, I would have been left wearing underpants!

When I reached the hotel, I saw about eighty people waiting in the shade of a huge mango tree. There was no waiting room for the interviewees. I provided the comic interlude, it seemed to me, because almost everyone was dressed in freshly laundered shirts and dhotis. A few wore ill-fitting pantsuits. I was the only one who had a suit on. I heard snickers and muttered comments about the "sahib"—a term used to refer to the white people.

At exactly 2:00 p.m., one of the locals officiating for the duo of officers called the first name on the list. For the first time, I realized the importance of having a surname beginning with A or B. N is quite down the list, and there were many Nairs. Nayars came even further down!

But what intrigued me was that the duration of each interview was quite short—hardly three minutes, some even shorter.

When my name was called, my heart missed a beat. Walking into the room was a physical relief, because there were two fans going, and for someone who had walked in the sun in someone else's shoes, stood for a long time, albeit under a mango tree, the change was very welcome.

I shall never forget the scene. Both the officers were dressed in suits, and when I walked in, upholstered in a white sharkskin jacket and blue woolen pants, starched white shirt, and a tie to match, there was this incredulous look on their faces! "Well, well, well," Ouseley said, "what do we have here? Do sit down. Would you like some tea?"

I was wondering how I would ever drink a cup of tea in three minutes or less without gulping it down. But I wanted to moisten my throat and so I said, "Yes, thank you."

Since I had applied for an English position, the discussion was mostly about English—reading habits, favorite authors, teaching methods, and such. Why do you like Somerset Maugham? Who wrote *How Green Was My Valley*? (I recall I made them laugh, because I did not pronounce the last name of the author "Llewellyn" correctly! It would take a trip to Wales to learn the correct pronunciation!) Can you recite a few lines from Wordsworth? (Easy, after all, because my father had me memorize "The Daffodils".) What did Dylan Thomas die of? (I had no idea. Alcoholism, Ouseley offered!)

The session went on for over fifteen minutes. It was as though they were actually enjoying the interview. When I walked out, everyone wanted to know why it took so long. What happened? What did they ask you?

Well, I was the only one selected from Thiruvananthapuram. Dealing with MacKinnon Mackenzie (the agents of the government), getting a passport, getting a brand new wardrobe, the very first visit to Mumbai, the very first cruise to Mombasa and the delightful train journey to Kampala...the reel runs fast.

Incidentally, the cabin trunk that I used for my first trip overseas is adorning my daughter's living room. It is a collectors' item, I guess; it still has stickers from P&O & BI, the cruise company, showing my cabin number.

Kampala and Uganda would be, I thought, a dream come true. But it was not to be.

"*What happens to a dream deferred? Does it dry up like a raisin in the* sun?" asked the American poet Langston Hughes.

Not necessarily, because one can dream again. We did.

CHAPTER FOUR

OH, CANADA

Kampala to Boyle, Alberta, Canada, via London, Mumbai, Calcutta, Tokyo, Vancouver, and Calgary was a very long and arduous haul, especially with a kid who was one year old.

The trip was not without incidents. We flew to London from Entebbe, *en route* to Mumbai. We arrived in London around seven in the morning. We checked into a hotel near the airport. I had some bank business to attend to, for which I had to go downtown. Nalini laid half asleep Nikku (my son) on the bed and went to the bathroom. When she returned the baby was gone.

Well, I don't need to describe the panic that ensued! The management was just about getting ready to call the police, when a cleaning lady reported that she had found a sleeping baby on the floor in one of the rooms, which had been recently vacated by a client. She was getting it ready for the next client when she discovered the baby.

Apparently what happened was that Nikku woke up to find that his mother was not in the room, and so proceeded to look for her. He did not go far when fatigue overtook him, and he walked through the next open door and promptly fell asleep on the floor.

Blame jet lag for all the drama, I guess!

The local member of the school board, Stan Zayezierski, met us in Athabasca, the County headquarters, and drove us to Boyle. We reached Boyle around 2:00 p.m. The car stopped in front of a very old building at the junction of two roads, the two main roads of the village as it turned out. The L-shaped building in the corner housed a restaurant, a six-room hotel upstairs, a Marshall Wells hardware store and a gas station. Across the road and the railway tracks there were two grain elevators, which I had seen only in pictures.

Stan said, "Well, here we are."

Nalini and I looked at each other. *What have we come to, where have we come to?* we thought.

I should mention, though, that we really did not know what to expect. We knew it was a small town. But how small is small? We arrived sometime in mid August in 1965. To say that we were a novelty to the Boylers would be an understatement. The community was already aware that an Indian had been hired to teach English in the school and that he was arriving from Africa!

I did not know that we had created a cognitive confusion among the people in Boyle. Indian meaning what? As you are, perhaps, aware, in Canada, one has to make a distinction between an

Indian and a man from India. These days, we are classified as South Asians; but in 1965, in Boyle, an Indian was a native Indian and they could have surmised that we belonged to a tribe they had never heard about!

What initial impressions we had created among the few people who had gathered when we stepped out of the car, I cannot tell. But for us, the day started in a very interesting manner.

When we left Africa, we were advised to pack large quantities of napkins (nappies) for the trip, because, our son was just over a year old. By the time we reached Boyle, we had almost exhausted our supply of nappies, even though we had replenished it in Tokyo. So I walked to the chemists. (The term "drug store" had not yet become part of our vocabulary.) The manager who had known all about us ahead of time was very pleasant and courteous and, when I asked for some napkins, he promptly produced a packet of four-inch squares with scalloped edges. I suspect there was a picture of a holly in one corner.

"No, no," I said, "I want something larger."

Of course. Out came dinner napkins. Obviously, there was lack of communication. So I resorted to using the universal language—theatre—and demonstrated what I would use the napkins for.

"Oh, you want diapers. Why didn't you say so? Of course we have them in plenty."

On my return to the hotel, I told Nalini that we had a major problem viz. a linguistic dissonance. We had to learn a new language—certainly a new vocabulary—and if possible, a new accent. We soon learned to use the word "boot" only to refer to footwear and not the storage space at the back of a car (in front, if you had a Volkswagen beetle).

It is only fair to say that the community warmly welcomed us and was very helpful in getting us settled. There was no house to rent, a fourplex was under construction and, hence, we were temporarily accommodated in a house trailer, pulled in from some farm and parked on a vacant lot of land near the school. We had never seen a trailer before! Obviously we had never lived in one, either. Temporary electrical connections were given.

1965 would turn out to be one of the coldest in the history of Alberta. Occasionally, the mercury fell below 50° Celsius. The change from balmy Kampala to freezing Boyle was something very hard to get used to. Yet the trailer was warm, even though it was freezing outside.

After supper one day in early January, I went to the school for a meeting. When I returned, around nine or so, I found the house (!) in darkness. Nalini had been ironing a few clothes and decided to make some tea to keep her insides warm. Suddenly, the fuse blew and plunged the trailer into darkness. No power meant no heat, of course. When I came back, I saw mother and child wrapped in blankets and cowered in a corner of the chesterfield. They were both crying. Nalini was, obviously, very angry and upset and demanded that we get out of the place the very next day.

I put them in the warm car. Not being very conversant with the mysteries of electrical connections, I had to drive to the house of the local electrician who reluctantly agreed to investigate the matter. I thought I heard him mumbling something about fuses. Yup, it was. He left with the warning that we should never use two appliances at the same time!

Of course, we did not leave the next day, or for that matter for the next six years! The county heard all about the horror story and expedited the construction of the fourplex, and we moved into our new digs sometime in early spring.

During winter, I was also introduced to the game of curling. I had never even heard of the game before coming to Boyle. But in smaller centres in Canada it is, of course, the prime pastime in the winter.

Stan, who was an avid curler, always tried to include a rookie in his team, and so he asked me to join. I tried to wriggle out of it, pleading ignorance, but he assured me that it was an easy game to learn and play. Also, it was great fun and would provide a very good opportunity to meet people, Stan promised.

So, I appeared one evening for the first match of the bonspiel (another new term). It turned out to be the very first game of the season, as well. I had a quick "learn to curl in five easy steps" session with Stan. He said among, other things, that I would be the lead. I protested. I said that I was in no position to lead anything, not knowing anything about the game. Well, that concern was soon put to rest because, I was told, that the lead is the person who starts the game and that the skip—possibly a short version of the nautical term skipper—would control the game. All I had to do was to throw the rock so that it reached the "house".

"Where is the house?" I asked ingenuously, because all I could see were three concentric rings at the end of the rink. Well, that problem was resolved in a hurry.

So I poised myself to "throw" a piece of rock weighing a ton, it seemed to me, when I was further instructed to my great relief that I only had to slide the rock, not really throw it.

Which I proceeded to do.

But Stan did not tell me that I should release the rock! So, much to the amusement of the spectators, there was this hugely embarrassed Indian at the end of a curling rock, sliding down a few meters! Needless to say the incident was mirthfully narrated at many parties through the season, each time getting further embellished a bit.

The very first year in Boyle, I thought I should try to do something I had never done before—direct a play. The community never had a theatre group. Many of the people had not even seen live theatre. Some of the culturally inclined people used to drive down to Edmonton, some ninety miles south, and take in a show mounted by the Citadel Theatre. So I formed two companies—one for the school (The Boyle Players) and the one for the adults (Boyle Community Theatre).

The idea of a theatre was a novelty and, hence, many people signed up. I chose *All My Sons* by Arthur Miller for the first production. Considering the "talent" I had to work with, I should say that the play was an unqualified success.

Boyle School was, unbeknownst to me, referred to as the graveyard of Principals. Within the previous four years of our arrival, the school had three principals, and I am not in a position to explain the problem. All I knew was that the life expectancy of a principal in Boyle was a maximum of two years. I suspect, though, that local politics played more than a small role. So the Board, in their wisdom, decided that an outsider, perhaps, might be able to reverse the trend and, in the fall of 1966, I was offered the job. It was with a great deal of trepidation that I accepted it.

I recall the first staff meeting. I was nervous, and the staff seemed somewhat apprehensive, as well. So I asked the honest question: what exactly does a Principal do? There was no quick response or any response for that matter. There was an amused expression on their faces. I assured them that I would support them as much as I could, work for their benefit, and deal with any professional issues they might have. I asserted that I was not prepared to "supervise" them, and they should do what they had been trained to do to the best of their ability. The needs and the interests of the students were paramount, I reminded them.

Administrative challenges in a new place, and other related issues, compelled me to give up the task of running two drama companies, and so I chose to concentrate on The Boyle Players. This company regularly put on performances and entered the Drama Festivals. In fact, their play *Birdbath* by Leonard Melfi won the Regional Award for the best school production in 1969. The play went to the Provincial competition. Edward Wolak and Darlene Bencharsky who played the lead roles were both picked for the best performance in a male and female role, respectively.

One of the first things I did in the school was to bring a little British flavor, and that was to divide the junior and senior high school into "Houses". Activities during the noon-hour recess were not structured, and many students opted to go to the town for coffee, smokes, or whatever. If the weather was very bad, they went to the gym and played basketball or volleyball. Thus, a House System was introduced, and three houses were "built". Each house had students from grades seven to twelve. They competed in sporting events, including curling. But there were competitions in such events as one act drama, poetry recitations, elocution, handicrafts, baking, etc. Each House had a teacher as their leader. The winning House collected points in the various events, and there was a bulletin board, which displayed the cumulative total for each House. I got the local mayor and GM car dealer to donate an enormous trophy, almost three feet high. The non-believers got converted, and the inter-house competitions during the noon-hour recess became something to look forward to, especially during the winter.

During the second year of my tenure, we got an addition to the existing building. A Home Economics room and a new gym were added. The old gym was converted into an Industrial Arts room.

The incredulous expression on the faces of the students when I announced that girls could enroll in Industrial Arts classes and the boys could enroll in Home Economics was so palpable that I relish reminiscing about it even today. I told the boys that, one day, they might be required to prepare a meal for themselves or others. To the girls, I said that some day they might have to fix an unsteady shelf or stop a drip from a leaky faucet. Needless to say, the experiment was highly successful. One girl took to automotives with great interest.

Another innovation that I tried happened as the result of a discipline problem. The teacher of social studies had given the grade eleven students a reading assignment, followed by a written one. One student, an extremely bright fellow, finished his work with about fifteen minutes to spare and was working on his math lesson. The teacher happened to walk by, and seeing the student engrossed in mathematics, rather than his beloved social studies, got hot under the collar and booted him out of the class and sent him to the Principal. Obviously. That is what teachers do: send the "problem" students to the Principal.

It was easy to learn that the student had not done anything *wrong*. What was at stake was the ego of the teacher. I am not sure how I settled this by not offending basic justice, which every student deserves and, by saving the face of a teacher, who was obviously wrong.

This set me thinking. Why on earth should students be tied to policies that are not flexible? During the span of an hour, framed by what is called a "timetable", are the students really spending the whole time in fruitful pursuits? If a student has satisfied the requirements set out by the teacher or the curriculum, why should the system deny freedom to the student to do whatever he or she wants as long as the act is educationally relevant and not unlawful? Unless, of course, the teacher is lecturing the whole hour.

Thus, the "Open Campus" project was born. I called a meeting of the high school teachers and floated the idea. In a nutshell, the teacher, on the first day of the week, would either teach a concept and/or give an assignment to be finished within a specified time. How fast the students accomplished the task was left to the student, but it had to be before the next assignment was given. The teacher would be available during the whole period every week if the student needed help. When not doing the assignment, the student could spend time anywhere within the premises of the school—in the library, the common room, the field, the shop, the home economics room, or wherever. But they had to report first to the teacher before going anywhere.

The common room had a ping pong table, scrabble, a card table, dominoes, magazines, etc.

Obviously, the common room was filled to capacity during the first few weeks of the experiment. A few of the students lost their privileges for abusing their newly acquired freedom. But soon, things got normal, and the students fell into a kind of routine. A few senior students who were planning on enrolling in the education faculty at the university even volunteered to help teachers in the elementary grades.

Of course, I had to get prior permission from the Superintendent. I was lucky to have a boss who was way ahead of the times. But I was not prepared for a visit from the officials of the Department of Education. The first question they asked me was, "We were told that there is a mess here. What is it? Where is it?" Then I knew that someone had squealed on me directly to the Department. I was quite surprised that they had not told the Superintendent about their visit! I said that there was no mess, as far as I knew, and they were at liberty to wander around and discover it themselves.

They saw some very important and interesting things. A boy was working on the lathe in the workshop when he was supposed to be present in the mathematics class. He was making a surprise birthday gift for his father. Another student who was scheduled to be in the English class was quietly pouring over his biology textbook. The kids enjoyed the freedom and the teachers were not tied to a rigid schedule. They had more time to prepare lessons, mark papers, and so on. They also had the opportunity to give one-on-one sessions to students who needed extra help. The officials of the Ministry of Education were very happy with what they saw.

By now, local political problems were raising their collective heads. This was inevitable, especially because I was foreign in every sense of the word. Also, I was changing the status quo. Change is an uncomfortable thought, especially if one is dubious about the ability to embrace change. The chief antagonist was a local man, who taught junior high school. I did not realize that he had been secretly harboring the desire to be the head of the school. But the Board would not have appointed him for many reasons that are not relevant here. Suffice it to say that he began to make my job difficult. Even though he left town for another jurisdiction, I thought it was time for us to leave. Also, Boyle was not the place to raise our two kids. We thought that they deserved a larger center with better educational opportunities and cultural activities. Grande Prairie Regional College in northern Alberta had a vacancy in the English department. I applied for the job, I got it, and in August 1971, I moved to Grande Prairie—population 13,000.

Grande Prairie was obviously a larger place. It is the largest center in the Peace River region. It had a reputation of supporting a vibrant arts community. The schools had a great music program.

The community had a very active theatre group. It was the cultural capital, as it were, of the Peace River region.

We stayed in Grande Prairie for thirty-nine years.

CHAPTER FIVE

THE PRODUCTIVE YEARS

The thirty-nine years in Grande Prairie, Alberta, from 1971 to 2010, were the longest we have ever lived at a stretch in one place; and during this time many things happened to me, so that in the interests of clarity, I am going to divide this chapter into three parts: my involvement in theatre, my long tenure in the post secondary system, and my stint with the United Nations and The Canadian Executive Services Organization.

Involvement in Theatre

When I applied for the job at Grande Prairie Regional College, I was somewhat skeptical, because most post-secondary institutions were reluctant to appoint non-native speakers to teach English.

And I probably might not have got the job either, had not a friend in the faculty suggested to the Chairman that he should at least give me the benefit of an interview and not dismiss the application because I was an Indian. Admittedly, I had lost the clipped accent that I had meticulously cultivated while in the colonial service. However, it appears that I had impressed the selectors.

I was quite excited that I would be able to get into the classroom again, because, as Principal, my teaching load was reduced to one course. The same thing happened in Uganda, as well. When I became Senior Master, I taught only three classes a day, instead of the normal five.

But more than teaching, I was looking forward to getting involved in some serious theatre work.

My very first involvement in theatre was in India, of course, and it was the result of a blatant act of nepotism! My father was an active member of an association of Nairs, called The Nair Sahodara Samajam (NSS). This is an organization that provides help to the Nair community during betrothal ceremonies, weddings, funerals, and big family events. They also developed a foundation from which they would subsidize the education of poor Nair boys and girls who could not afford the cost of textbooks. It was a statewide volunteer organization, and each town had its own branch or chapter. The NSS opened libraries in rural communities. Eventually, they would start schools, and even colleges that offered graduate and post-graduate courses. They would also acquire a great deal of political clout.

One of the branches in our capital city had, among other things, taken up the task of converting Malayalam classic novels into plays and staging them. The elite in the city always looked forward to the annual production of the NSS. The company would, as it turned out, spawn the growth of many actors who eventually became famous throughout the state by their performances for other companies and even in movies.

I believe I was eight years old, and the play that particular year required a boy to appear on stage and say, "Sir, they have arrived", or something to that effect. My father was an amateur director/ actor, though I cannot recall ever seeing him on the stage. But he cast me in the role and I gave him assurances that I could pull it off!

The theatre groups, then, did not have the luxury of dress rehearsals and technical rehearsals. The opening night was the first time the company performed on the stage. We also had something called "footlights" to illuminate the stage. Fresnels, long throws, spots, and other instruments were unknown. The footlights would be anchored to the apron of the stage.

On cue, kindly supplied with a prod by someone backstage (which hurt, incidentally) I ran on to the stage, looked at the vast blackness in front of me, squinted at the lights and froze. The man opposite whom I was playing, apparently tried to prompt me with a question of some kind, but there was no thaw in sight. So the gentleman (!) put his arm around me and pinched me so hard that, instead of yelping, I stammered out my "line" (much to the amusement of the audience) and went backstage and cried for a while.

My father would immediately pronounce judgment that I had no sense of theatre. Maybe he did not mean it, and I would prove him wrong.

In those days, men played the roles of women. Ladies from "decent" families did not go on the stage! I did want to pursue theatre as a hobby, for sure, perhaps as a career, but my height or lack of it, mitigated against getting leading or major roles. (I know, I know, Stanislavsky did say that there are no small roles, only small actors!) I was not a bad looking lad, and soon I got invited to play girls and, later, until I left for Uganda, women's roles. We had great make-up artists. I believe I must have been involved in over two dozen plays.

In 1946, during my third year at university, Shakespeare's Macbeth was required reading. As it happened, a British company called Shakespeareana was touring India and had announced one performance of Macbeth in our hometown. Our professor strongly advised us to see the show. The charismatic husband and wife team of Geoffrey and Laura Kendall headed the company. They came to India during the war to entertain British troops. But after the war, they stayed on and joined the well-known company in Mumbai—The Prithvi Theatre.

Macbeth was an eye opener. First of all, I had never seen a performance by a foreign troupe. This group had a small cast—

thirteen as I recall—performing a play that required several dozen actors. Obviously, several roles were "doubled" and much was left to the imagination of the audience.

From the actor's point of view, I observed that something else was different; and that was the "behavior" of the actors on the stage. For the first time, I noticed that the actors were talking to one another. We were used to—indeed asked to—stand at a quarter profile, and look at the audience as much as possible (but not always), and we were roundly chastised if we did not. The notion was that, by looking away, the audience would not hear the dialogue, which, of course, is the essence of the play. Perhaps the Indian directors were trying to emulate Greek traditions. I don't know for sure.

Of course, I would notice again the conceptual differences, the style, and clever placement of actors on the stage—called *blocking* in theatre parlance—when I went to see shows in London.

My last performance in India was in early 1955, though by then, strictures on women participating on the stage were being loosened.

I did not have much of a chance to do theatre in Uganda. I acted in a play in Malayalam mounted by the Kairali Association. I probably could have been involved in more, but in Kampala, we did not have qualified make up artists, and the women were reluctant to go on the stage. We were, thus, forced to look for plays that required an all male cast, and this was not easy.

I also assisted in the staging of a school production—a Swahili translation of *Julius Caesar* by Julius Nyerere, a schoolteacher, who would eventually become the Prime Minister of Tanzania. I can't say it was much of a success. I also had decided that, as far as I was concerned, any theatre involving children would be theatre for children and not by children.

So, it was with a great deal of anticipation that I looked forward to getting deeply involved in theatre in Grande Prairie. Of course, I did not know anyone in the theatre community. One day, I was chatting about my hobby and deep desire with Art Ross, another instructor in the English faculty. I just wanted to know whom I should contact in the community. Art was a big man and had a striking resemblance to Oscar Wilde. He gave one of his characteristic guffaws and said the Grande Prairie Little Theatre— GPLT—was a very close-knit organization; it was a very private club, and they would not even give me the time of day! My skin tone wouldn't help either, he added.

"Then we should start our own theatre group," I said.

Thus, The College Players was born.

Art Ross was teaching *The Ecstasy of Rita Joe* as part of the Canadian Literature course, and he suggested that I debut the company with that play. I agreed, not realizing the colossal challenges that were awaiting me!

The play, which is a seminal work in the history of Canadian theatre, was written by George Ryga who, coincidentally, was born in the county of Athabasca where Boyle is. The story, told in songs, montages, and tableaux, is about issues relating to aboriginal people. Specifically, it deals with an aboriginal woman who goes to the city to find freedom from the limitations of life on the reservation. She ends up dead, which does not deter three white men from engaging in necrophiliac rape. Ross told me it is a play for all seasons, for all people.

Grande Prairie in the 70's was a very conservative town. A typical GPLT season consisted of two plays—one in the fall, usually a comedy, along the lines of Neil Simon, and a spring musical like *Fiddler on the Roof.* They also competed in the Adult One Act Drama Festival. They had never ventured into anything controversial.

The news that the new instructor at the college was going to put on a show where there would be actual rape of a dead Indian woman, performed on the stage, was understandably received with mixed reactions! Some of my friends asked me to withdraw the production. A few others suggested that I look for another job!

Well, I did not lose my job; Grande Prairie sat up and took note of me. I must say that I was welcomed with warmth by the theatre community. In fact, that year, GPLT invited me to direct *All My Sons* by Arthur Miller.

Rita Joe was a success, considering the challenges. But there is a story to tell—a story which, I want to believe, is my crowning achievement in my very long stint in the theatre in Canada and elsewhere.

The play requires an Indian woman, of course; but an equally important role is that of the chief of the reservation. Chief Dan George played this role when the play first opened in Vancouver. (The Chief would, in 1971, receive the Order of Canada.) It turned out to be difficult to find a suitable person for the role, and I was about to call off the show. I was not prepared to make a white man look like an Indian. I had read about the controversy in the United States and elsewhere about white people playing Othello.

Then someone told me that in the Faculty of Continuing Education there was a Métis student by the name Ira Mitchell who was trying to upgrade his English and Mathematics to the grade-nine level so that he could go to Edmonton and get trained as a butcher. He had dropped out of grade seven many years ago. He almost looked the part—middle aged, with noticeable Indian features. But he stammered horribly. All the same, I approached him.

He was predictably irritated that I would ask him to go on stage, knowing fully well that he stuttered.

"Are you trying to make me look stupid in front of a bunch of people?" I recall him asking me.

I assured him that it was not the intention at all; but would he at least read the script? He agreed, and the next day, he brought the book back. He liked the play, he said. He felt that it must be done but said that he wouldn't be part of the production.

After a great deal of cajoling, he finally agreed to play the role. I had already warned the rest of the cast that they would have to be infinitely patient with Mitchell, and they were. The rehearsals were painful, to say the least. Timing went out of the window; the players would patiently wait for Mitchell to finish his line, so that they could get on with theirs.

Finally, it was opening night. The story was out that there was going to be rape on the stage, and the auditorium, which in fact was the gymnasium of the local high school, was filled to capacity.

When the Chief first appears, he gives a beautiful lyrical piece about nature, the butterflies, the birds, flowers, and how a reservation could be a beautiful place to live in. Mitchell was alone on the stage. Nothing happened for what appeared to be an eternity. He blinked at the lights, took a very deep breath and spoke…without a stutter!

He has not stuttered since![6]

He would go on to finish requirements for his matriculation, and eventually acquire a Masters degree in Social Work and, the last I knew, he was working as a counselor for the aboriginal people in the Peace Region!

---

6   It is strangely coincidental that the 2011 Oscar for best male actor went to Colin Firth for his portrayal of the stammering king in *The King's Speech*. When I saw the movie, I was, naturally, reminded of *Rita Joe*, because I experienced first-hand the pain, disappointment, anger, and frustration that a stutterer feels when trying to speak in public.

❦

The College Players would eventually become a strong presence in the city and the region. None of the actors were trained, and so I decided to start an acting class—not for credit, just for fun. The response was enthusiastic. I believe I had about twenty students during the first year.

In 1973, I was appointed as Chairman of Continuing Education, thus, again, reducing my teaching load! But I had more time to pursue theatre. I regularly directed plays for GPLT, and the College Players produced at least one major play every year—sometimes two. In addition, my plays entered the Drama festivals—regional and provincial. I went slightly off mainstream, meaning the choice of plays was not typical community theatre fare. *Whose Life is it Anyway?*, *The Runner Stumbles*, *An Enemy of the People*, *Children of a Lesser God*, *The Shadow Box*, *Extremities*, *The Visit*, and *Art* are a few of the plays that I consider successful. The attractive feature, for me, at any rate, was that the company consisted of college and community people.

I am often asked which of the plays I had done was the best or my favorite. I have not been able to answer the question, because, to a director, the play is like a child. The director brings the page to the stage, makes something inanimate into something that breathes with life. It is like his or her baby, and every play is equally valuable, important, exciting! Having said that, *Children of a Lesser God*, I would say, was the most challenging because the script dealt with hearing and speech impaired people. In fact, the playwright, Mark Medoff, had a strict requirement that the leading roles be played only by people who are challenged in both areas.

As early as 1973, my intention was to elevate drama to credit status in the Grande Prairie Regional College curriculum. I was happy to note that the immediate response was generally good, and the University of Alberta approved a couple of courses. This number would increase, as the years went by. Today, the college boasts of a two-year diploma program in Drama, with the potential to transfer *in toto* to the third year drama at the University.

The College Players provided the lab for the students in drama. I proudly say that many of the students have gone on to professional work in the theatre, and many others who became lawyers, doctors, and such, fondly remind themselves and me that they were able to overcome their innate shyness and gain confidence by taking drama courses (see Cliff Mitchell's letter in the Postscript).

In 1975, I was appointed Chairman of Fine Arts—a vast department, including visual arts, dance, music, and a small drama department. In 1979, I attempted a major production—*Jesus Christ Superstar.* We had a great orchestra, comprised mostly of members of the music department; we had a large cast who did extraordinarily well for an amateur production.

J. C. Superstar would be a landmark production in another sense. It was only two weeks into rehearsals when I realized that there was a certain amount of resentment about the production, especially among some of the fundamentalist groups in the community. The Catholic Church was very supportive; in fact, for the Hosanna scene, they got me palm leaves all the way from Galilee.

The most vocal critic of the production was The Peace River Bible Institute. In those days, every Sunday, they had a radio program for an hour. Two weeks before the opening, the pastor, a man called Mclean, gave notice that the sermon the following week would be very important to the church and Christians everywhere, and he exhorted everyone to tune in. That particular Sunday, the pastor literally ripped the play apart, taking lines out of context and giving it an interpretation that could have been considered offensive.

For instance, in one song, Mary says, "He is a man; he's just a man..." The pastor thundered, "Here is a show that dares to call our Lord *just* a man; and the affront is compounded by the fact that the show is being directed by a Hindu. This is a calculated attempt to smear our Lord and our religion..."

The show was an unqualified success, and it ran for nine sellout performances, considering the city had only around 20,000 people.

In 2006, I did *Superstar* again. This time, the company consisted of over a hundred people. It was my swan song. Beginning with my dismal childhood performance in India in 1936, I probably had been involved in one capacity or another in over one hundred and fifty productions.

Rita Joe and *Superstar* changed the mindset of the community. And, as the Chairman of Fine Arts, I had the freedom and the funds to try various projects. Two of them are particularly noteworthy, in my opinion.

One was the starting of a group called Theatrix—a company that presented plays for children.

Earlier, I had mentioned that I had advocated theatre for children and not by children. In 1961, while in London, I had occasion to attend a workshop given by Brian Way, who was crusading in British schools on what was then a novel idea called Theatre in Education. He drew a subtle distinction between "theatre" and "drama". Theatre, he maintained, was largely concerned with communication between actors and an audience. Drama was concerned with the experience by participants, irrespective of any function of communication to an audience. Theatre is, undoubtedly, achievable with a few—a very small minority—but drama is concerned with a majority, and there is no child who cannot do drama.

Or so his argument went.

I did not pay much attention to it at that time or until 1965, when I arrived in Boyle. During the first year, sometime in November or so, I heard teachers talking about the Christmas show and who was doing what and so on. Having started a drama club already, I was curious about the class productions. On inquiring, I learned that it was an annual event, where each class put on a "show" before the Christmas break. There would be a noon-hour show for the students and an evening show for the parents and dignitaries.

So, on the day of the show, the Grade One students came on stage, stood in a line, and did a piece of choral work—a song of some kind. I am not sure what punishment was meted out to the girl who, while singing, was seeking out her parents in the audience and, when she was successful, surreptitiously waved at them. Grade Two also did something similar. Grade Three to Six had a "play", a few students playing roles, wearing "costumes", boys with moustaches drawn across their upper lips, pretending to be old men.

The next day, I asked the teachers how they picked the cast for the plays. I don't think I got a proper answer—something to the effect that those picked to be in the cast were smarter than the others! I asked if "the others" would have felt left out, and whether it would have damaged their self-esteem in any way.

"Well, one cannot find a play for thirty students," one of them retorted.

"True," I said, "but you can do drama instead of theatre."

Is there a difference?

The question was genuine, incredulous. I said that there was but did not expand on it. The following year, I could have used my authority as Principal and tried to do some drama in the classroom; but I thought I would be imposing on the teachers and forcing them to do something they had no training in. Also, it would have encroached on an already crowded curriculum. So I had to be satisfied with the development of The Boyle Players.

Back to Grande Prairie. I had the opportunity of offering an evening course for teachers—a course designed for those who had little or no training in drama and were enthusiastic about introducing it in the classroom. Though it started off as an exercise in professional development, later I would get accreditation for this course, and it would become a popular option for B.Ed. students.

Theatrix was a great success. The company consisted of doctors, lawyers, teachers, and students from the drama and music departments. We wrote original scripts based on fables, folklore (Nanabush stories) and, sometimes, on national and international news stories. We visited the local schools during the noon-hour break. We had two shows—one for grades one to three and another for grades four to six. During weekends, we toured the region. Eventually, time or lack of it became an issue. A local impresario tried to run with it, but he could not sustain it for more than three months. The region still does not have a viable theatre for children.

The second project that I started was an "Evening with…" series that The College Players mounted. The first production was called *An Evening with the Greeks.* It was basically "Readers Theatre". Greek food was served, followed by selected scenes from Greek plays. We had evenings with Shaw, Shakespeare, Sheridan, Chekhov, and Wilde.

In 1979, I was granted sabbatical leave for one academic year, but I decided to get an early start in the spring and go on until the following summer, and thus squeeze in six semesters in any university of my choice. Broadway beckoned me, and hence, I enrolled in a combined MA/ Ph.D. program in theatre at the New York University (NYU).

Without doubt, those were the best and most rewarding twelve months of my academic life. I don't think I need to list all the various choices for entertainment there are in the Big Apple. I had access to a veritable feast of performing arts.

But the most exciting thing was, of course, the drama school itself, the staff of which contained giants like Richard Schechner, Alan Schneider, Charles Ludlum, and Barbara Kirshenblatt-Gimblett, among others.

One of the professors, Dr. Jean Wright, had an apartment on Fifth Avenue, five minutes away from NYU. She also had a home in Nyack, New York. That particular year, she was going on sabbatical herself, and she wondered if I would like to rent her apartment for a year. I jumped at the offer, and so the potential problem of housing, which could be a serious one in New York, was solved easily.

But the most important thing that would help me in my career happened quite accidentally. Jean invited me over to spend a weekend in Nyack, and in the evening, she casually mentioned that supper would be at her neighbor Helen's house. Only when I went there did I realize that "Helen" was none other than the great Helen Hayes! Obviously, her guests were people connected with theatre—actors, directors, critics. One of the invitees was a man called Harry Davies, whom some of my generation might remember as the old guy promoting Pepsi Cola in commercials. He was a member of The Actors Studio run by Lee Strasberg. Of course, you get admitted to this prestigious institution, only if you are a professional actor or an actor in training. But the Studio occasionally admitted "observers" who were allowed to sit in on some of the sessions. Harry used his clout and got me in. (The Actors Studio is not a school, but an active studio for the members.)

Every Friday for two hours, I was treated to some of the finest theatrical experiences of my life. During these days, acknowledged professionals like Robert De Niro, Dustin Hoffman, Joanne Woodward, Julie Harris, and Ellen Burstyn would come prepared to do a half-hour scene from a play. The scene usually involved two people. After the performance, Strasberg and, sometimes, Elia Kazan would critique the production—sometimes brutally—and one learned a lot from those sessions. The established actors did this regularly, whenever time permitted, to hone their skills. I was surprised that they would put up with Strasberg's stinging comments, but they knew that they were listening to a master. They welcomed the critique, which is why they came there in the first place.

But watching the exercise was immensely useful to me, and I was able to improve my own skills in directing. It was during these sessions that I got a reasonable grasp of the famed Method Acting. I had read about it, of course, but the experience of how exactly it is practiced was something that had eluded me. Watching actors actually employ the method gave me a clearer idea of the system. It also helped me to appreciate the work of Marlon Brando, Paul Newman, Eli Wallach, Al Pacino, and other notable alumni of The Actors Studio.

My post graduate work at NYU was going to be concentrated on rituals, masks, and their relationship to theatre; and during this process, I was introduced to a rather esoteric discipline in theatre called "Performance Theory", which, of course, went to the roots of theatre in various cultures. Richard Schechner is the world's leading expert in the theory, and I consider myself extremely fortunate to have had classes from him. He was also my mentor. Even before I went to New York, I had, in my mind, decided that if I ever did any post-graduate work at all, it would have something to do with masks and rituals and, for that reason, I went to Bali several times to do research in Balinese theatre. I already had a reasonable grounding in *Kathakali*.[7] In fact, I had no choice because my father would insist that I go to some of the performances, which were famous for their masks and notorious for the length of the production, which averaged four hours. It is also unique in the sense that, even today, female roles are played by men.

During one of these visits to Bali, I decided to go to India and, while I was in Mumbai, my cousin, a professional actor himself, asked me if I would be interested in directing *The Shadow Box* for Burjor Patel Productions. This company is well known for producing plays in English. My cousin was aware that I had already done the play in Grande Prairie, Burjor was looking for a director, I happened to be in Mumbai…

It was the first time that I had directed a company of professionals. Here, I mean a company where actors were paid. I always maintain that the only difference between amateurs and professionals should be that one gets paid and the other does not, and the terms do not necessarily reflect quality. I have seen professionals putting on mediocre shows and amateurs mounting brilliant productions. Think Ottawa Little Theatre![8]

---

7   Kathakali is a highly stylized classical Indian dance-drama noted for its attractive make-up of characters, elaborate costumes, and well-defined body movements. It originated in Kerala during the 17th century.

8   Professional in style, traditional in tone, Ottawa Little Theatre is the longest-running community theatre in Canada. It is a charitable not-for-profit, volunteer-based organization, almost a hundred years old. It is financially dependent on subscribers and their donations.

The Shadow Box is about three cancer patients in their terminal stages and how the immediate families deal with the situation. Powerful stuff!

The Indian Cancer Society sponsored the opening night, and the Governor was the chief guest. At curtain, a sellout crowd at the National Center for the Performing Arts in Mumbai stood up in the most spontaneous standing ovation I have ever seen.

While I was the Chairman of Fine Arts, the economy of Grande Prairie went through the boom/bust cycle. When a government is unable to adequately fund educational institutions, the first thing to go on the chopping block is the arts—widely maligned as "frill" subjects! Grande Prairie Regional College had the same fate. The college got a new president who inherited a deficit budget. While she actively supported a new Nursing program, the Fine Arts department went under the scalpel, because she was determined to balance the books and vowed that there would be no more deficits under her watch. The Department of Continuing Education was decimated. This was a shame, because with the cuts, many non-credit, general-interest courses also disappeared from the college calendar.

All of a sudden, I was looking at a staff of three in music (from seven), two in visual arts (from five), and zero in drama (from two). The auditorium would eventually be closed and, with that act, a Technical Director and two assistants got their walking papers. I was kept on staff to head the anemic department, but more importantly to write a proposal for new funding for a Visual and Performing Arts Diploma Program. The hope was that if the proposal were approved, the Fine Arts department would rise again like the Phoenix.

Two years later, the department would be resurrected. But all the cutting and rebuilding also destroyed the culture of the department, along with morale, and I chose to step down as the head of the department.

Abbotsford in British Columbia and St. Albert in Alberta had active theatres and both of them were looking for a General Manager, and I applied for both. I got the job in St Albert. But, meanwhile, I also saw that Fairview College was seeking a senior administrator to run their program in High Level in the northern region. The salary was great, the job description challenging, and so I threw my hat in. After a somewhat rigorous interview, Fairview gave me the job. I rejected St Albert and, in 1986, I took over as Northern Regional Director of Fairview College.

I served in that position for two years, after which the UN hired me as a consultant.

On the eve of my departure from Grande Prairie for High Level, GPLT decided to hold a general meeting of the members and friends. They honored me with a life membership. During the function, the president of GPLT said, among other things, that "Sukumar made theatre happen in Grande Prairie."

I suppose in a way I did. Starting The College Players which became a viable alternative to GPLT, starting Theatrix, which is still a grand idea for someone to develop, training several hundred teachers and B.Ed students in introducing drama in the classroom, directing landmark shows—especially what can be loosely called "message plays"—all these add up to something substantial, I guess.

But one of the kudos that I cherish most came as a result of the effort of The Theatre Network in Edmonton, Alberta. They, with the support of the government, decided to honor one hundred theatre practitioners during the millennium year 2005. For reasons that I do not know, the actual award could not be given until 2006. It was called *Theatre 100*. The blurb said, "Awarded to one hundred theatre practitioners who have made significant contribution to the development of theatre in Alberta during the last hundred years."

It humbled me that I was in the company of some of the giants in the business. I am particularly thrilled that, in the commemoration book, I share the pages with the illustrious Thespian, the late John Neville. This was not because of any similarity between our efforts or our contribution to theatre. Taken in alphabetical order, Neville followed Nayar; that is all.

Involvement in the Post Secondary System

This section is meant to deal with my advancement in the post-secondary system. But a lot of it has already been covered tangentially in the previous section, and hence, this section will only complement it. I will attempt not to replicate any information already recorded.

First I want to mention that, during my career, all administrative appointments except the position of Regional Director at Fairview College had come as a result of nomination by the faculty or the head of the institution. And this included the position of Senior Master of English in Uganda.

I attribute this to several factors. I am basically a very organized person, and I think I have better than ordinary communication skills. I also have, what could be characterized as, mundane administrative skills. By this I mean what might appear to be pedestrian jobs like an intelligent filing system, the habit of responding promptly to correspondence and phone calls, meeting deadlines, addressing and, when possible, redressing issues raised by the colleagues under my care and paying special attention to the problems of students in the department. The importance of these cannot be overstated. I am also a "people person", and I want to think that I make people feel comfortable when they deal with me. It really takes a lot of aggravation for me to lose my cool. Perhaps the fact that I have been highly successful in the classroom—be it in India, Uganda, Wales, or Canada might also have contributed to my advancement.

My first administrative job in Grande Prairie was, as I've already mentioned, as the Chairman of Continuing Education. This was a rather amorphous department. Basically, it catered to upgrading adult students to enable them to go to Trade Schools and Universities. The department also had its share of non-credit, general interest courses. My wife was an instructor in this department and was in charge of Reading. She had taken several courses in this subject while we were in London. In fact, in Grande Prairie, she started a very sophisticated Reading Lab for the students. Until it got accreditation, Drama was also offered under this department.

One of the things I am particularly proud of is that I started an upgrading program in the Peace River Correctional Institution. Among the many incarcerated people, there were some who were quite intelligent, but who got on the wrong side of the law for one reason or another. Sometimes, the harsh conditions in the jail made them think clearly, and they sought to *clean up their act*, as the vernacular goes. One of the obvious things to do was to upgrade their level of education, there.

Until the college stepped in, such inmates had recourse only to correspondence courses offered by the Department of Education in Alberta. In the mid-seventies, the Institution had a sensitive warden who welcomed my offer to start a full-fledged upgrading program at the site. Of course, I had to go through complicated bureaucratic hoops and overcome unreasonable obstacles imposed by the Solicitor General, but I am happy to say that I was able to start the program.

My role in the development of a drama program in the college, especially during my tenure as Chairman of Fine Arts, has been dealt with already. During this time, the Minister of Culture appointed me to serve as a member of the Alberta Foundation for the Performing Arts. It was the mandate of the Foundation to disburse a portion of the proceeds from lotteries, to performers and performing arts organizations, to promote their work, enhance training, and underwrite tours within and outside the province. I held this position for three years.

During my stint as head of Fine Arts, I also discovered that I had skills as an impresario! First, I helped bring the great Victor Borge to Grande Prairie. It was surprisingly easy to mount a large sixty-eight-piece orchestra because, when musicians in the region heard about the privilege of playing for Borge, they came in droves! In fact, we had to hold auditions to pick the right people and the right combination, as required by the great man!

After the success with Borge, I set my sights on Danny Kaye. I had heard that he was coming to Vancouver, and hence, it was easy to get him over. He was willing to come but, unfortunately, he cancelled the Vancouver commitment because he suddenly was asked by UNICEF to go to the Far East on a special assignment. I also realized that such ventures demanded a lot of attention, time, and patience, and I was convinced that, while the project was great, it needed a full-time person.

During a time of austerity, it is insane to ask the President for money to fund a new position—especially in theatre. However, I did, and I was given permission to hire a person on a trial basis on condition that there would be sufficient revenue produced to underwrite the cost of operation of the theatre. This I did and the department brought in many famous acts like The Nylons, The Canadian Brass, The Royal Winnipeg Ballet, Tommy Banks, and Liona Boyd.

In 2008, I was admitted to the roster of Emeriti of Grande Prairie Regional College. The Fine Arts department also announced an annual scholarship in my name, to be awarded to an outstanding student in drama.

In High Level, I had the responsibility of administering twelve Adult Basic Education Centers. And I got the opportunity, for the first time, to deal with the education problems of adult Native Indians.

Two months into my tenure, I got a call from the principal of the school in a township called Assumption. This is a Federal Reservation and, as such, the school there was under federal jurisdiction. The principal wondered if I would lend him a typewriter! I was amused by his request, and so, naturally, I asked him what happened to his. It had broken down, and he had no permission to get it repaired locally. According to federal policy, he had to ship it to Ottawa, more than 2550 miles away, to get it fixed and, if not fixable, a requisition could be sent for purchasing a new one! The whole operation would have taken a minimum of six months, he added. Hats off to bureaucrats who drum up such policies!

Another very amusing incident happened while I was in High Level. Fairview College is well known for three programs: lawn maintenance, Harley Davidson motorbike maintenance, and beekeeping. For the beekeeping course they get students from overseas.

One day, the President called me to say that ten people had arrived from Dar es Salaam, the capital of Tanzania, to enroll in the beekeeping program. Since I had lived in East Africa, he thought that I might like to meet them. This I did and further invited them to spend a day in High Level.

I knew that the East Africans love curry, and I thought I would cook some for supper. The student counsellor in the college offered her trailer and moose meat to cook. Her husband was a keen hunter, and they had plenty of meat in the freezer. I also thought that moose meat would be a novelty for the Tanzanians.

When supper was served, I announced that the main ingredient in the curry was moose meat. When they started the meal, I thought there was some reluctance in eating the curry. Though they had reasonable helpings of the dish, they appeared to be avoiding it, pushing it to one side of the plate. I did not know what to make of it. After a while, one of them asked me in Swahili if I could clarify something. They did not want to offend the host and hence he was speaking in Swahili. What he wanted to know was how many mice had to be caught to produce so much curry! He, of course, thought that "moose" was a (possibly Canadian) plural form of "mouse"!

I could not help bursting into laughter, and the hostess wanted to know what the hilarity was all about. I asked her husband if he had a picture of a moose. He did. I showed the Africans the picture and explained what a moose really was. Obviously relieved, they attacked the curry with a great deal of enthusiasm.

◈

I had many other rewarding experiences in High Level. One was the starting of a course in cooking. I hired a chef and enrolled thirteen students, ten of whom were Native Indians.

Of course, I also *had* to start a drama group, and, of course, it would be called The High Level Players! The first production mounted by the company was a play that GPLT had already done in Grande Prairie, *The Gin Game.* This is a two-hander, and I reprised the role I had played. Before the show, the hundred or so people who attended were treated to a sumptuous supper prepared by the cooking class. I had three *Evening with series* as well.

I also got the opportunity of being the morning man for the local radio station in High Level. I gave a half-hour broadcast every Wednesday.

I want to believe that I had a very successful tenure in the post-secondary system in Alberta—by any standard.

Involvement with the UN and CESO

UN

Mongolia

In the summer of 1989, I had to go to New York again to tidy up some of my course work and get a head start on my dissertation. Even when I was a regular student, occasionally I used to spend Saturday afternoons in the UN building, which has a restaurant/ bar facing the river. It is a quiet place to sip a beer and read…and watch people. After all, over a hundred and fifty countries were represented then, and I saw a bewildering variety of people belonging to different ethnic groups and heard an equally bewildering number of tongues! One day, during that particular trip, when I was returning from the restaurant, I saw a large poster, which said something like "The UN Needs You, Apply to UNDP", etc.

Out of curiosity I jotted down the details and, on returning to Alberta, I wrote to them saying that I was interested. Within a month I got in the mail the longest application form I have ever seen in my life—eight pages! Among other things, I was required to write seven hundred words on why I wanted to join the UN and why I thought I would be suitable for serving the organization. I was also asked to give my views on selected conflicts around the world.

It took almost eighteen months before I got a response from them.

The first appointment was to Viet Nam, which at that time, I did not think was the safest place to be. I was somewhat reluctant to accept the offer; but I was also afraid that, if I did not, it would be a strike against me. I turned it down anyway. But my rejection had no negative repercussions, and within five weeks, I was sent on assignment to Mongolia in 1991.

Mongolia had been under Soviet control for over six decades. But the introduction of *perestroika* in the USSR by Gorbachev strongly influenced Mongolian politics, leading to the peaceful Democratic Revolution, the introduction of a multi-party system, and a market economy. The transition to a market economy was very rocky, and the early 1990s saw high inflation and food shortages.

A major project for helping the country to stabilize the free market economy was already in the works. To facilitate the process, the country required many "managers" who were conversant with Western economic and governance systems. The UNDP was requested by the government to assist the School of Administration and Management to accelerate the project and upgrade the expertise of the managers.

Gabriel Iglesias, a Filipino from Manila, led the project. He was also required to teach Principles of Management and Administration. My job was to make the mid-level and senior officers of the government proficient in the use of English.

The day when I was due to leave Canada for Mongolia, I was setting out the bags on the driveway to be loaded in the car. I went inside to get my briefcase, when I suddenly heard Scottish pipes being played right in front of the house. I rushed out to see what was happening, and I saw a parked car with both front doors open and Scottish pipe music blaring out of the speakers. Some of my neighbors, who were attracted by the sound, also appeared on the scene.

What happened was this. Dr. Torquhil Matheson, a very dear friend (and a Scot), had secretly found out from Nalini the time of my departure for the airport. He had parked his car a few houses away from ours and, when he saw the suitcases on the driveway, he brought his car up and started playing a cassette with Scottish pipe music. Apparently, where he came from, anyone who goes on a long trip needed to be "sent off" to the accompaniment of pipe music. Torquhil died a few years later, and his family honored me by asking me to give the eulogy at his funeral.

I left for Ulaanbaatar, the capital of Mongolia, in mid 1991. My flight would take me to Moscow via Toronto. It was the first time I had been to Moscow.

About an hour before take off, I saw a woman walk into the departure lounge with a small dog. I was curious as to what the dog was doing there! But curiosity turned into astonishment, when she boarded the plane with the canine snuggled in the crook of her arm. During take off, I believe she had the animal on her lap. She was sitting several rows behind me. In a short time, I saw the animal running up and down the aisle. It was yelping loudly, as well. And no one could do anything about it, because the passengers and the crew were "belted" to their seats! I would notice the same thing in Mongolia; passengers boarded planes with chickens, dogs, and cats.

I was received at the airport by Enkhbat who was also assigned to be my interpreter. We became very good friends.

Reading up about the country when I got the assignment and during briefings by the UN, I had gathered, among other things, that the predominant religion in Mongolia used to be Tibetan Buddhism, but Stalin had destroyed all the monasteries, except one in the capital and had killed all the monks. He had also burned all the scripture books.

Western countries, except the UK, did not have embassies, and the US had only a consulate. India had an embassy; so did Japan, complete with a medico and a pharmacy. Of course, China and all European countries of the communist bloc had full diplomatic representation. As a Canadian, I was asked to register with the British embassy. Its watering hole "The Steppe Inn" (a rather clever name, I thought) was the meeting place for all expatriates in Ulaanbaatar.

The staff of UNDP consisted of mostly Mongolians. There were also a couple of Filipinos and a lady from Myanmar. The Director was a Russian, though a career diplomat named Robert de Mule would replace him a few months later.

I had a comfortable enough apartment. It was reasonably well furnished, had a fridge and stove. But I soon realized that basic things like rice, sugar, and salt were sometimes difficult to get. Fresh vegetables were a rarity. There was no agriculture to speak of in or around Ulaanbaatar. The local people ate beef, lamb, horsemeat, cheeses, and bread. The Russians had their own store, but only Russians were allowed. There was a "Diplomatic Store" from where you could buy some of the foreign "basic" things—whatever was available—like Nescafe, chocolates, tea, and cigarettes. There was a one-hour photo service run by a Chinese person!

Foreign liquor was also available in the "Diplomatic Store", but for that, a person had to pay US dollars, which meant that the average Mongolian could not buy it. They liked foreign vodka and, whenever I went to the store, there would be a mass of people outside, willing to give me tugriks, the local currency, sometimes at ten times the official exchange rate, if I would buy for them whatever they wanted. These people could get very violent if you did not accede to their demands, and so, I always went with Enkhbat, who would be pressed into service as a bodyguard.

The locals drank a concoction called *aarak* made by fermenting mare's milk. It tastes like buttermilk gone bad. The restaurants did not serve typical Western food, and so, the menu was almost always Russo-Mongolian, though one could order an omelet or fried egg served with bread or Vietnamese rice, which, uncooked, looked like barley and when cooked turned into something with the consistency of porridge.

The people were very friendly. I thought, though, that they had lost their sense of identity. They lived in subsidized housing. Civil servants paid by the state staffed the stores. So no one was in any great hurry to sell you anything. Sales or no, they would get paid. There were no taxis in Ulaanbaatar. However, you could stop a car and, in most cases, the driver would take you to your destination for a few tugriks. The city had a fairly regular bus service. The Moscow-Beijing train runs through Mongolia.

UNDP was caught in the changes in Russia in a curious way. Our project was supplied with a Honda van, which was waiting to be picked up at Vladivostok. The authorities would not release it, because they said the government had changed and they did not have new regulations regarding such matters. My boss sent me to negotiate with the Russians and release the car. We found the van in a box. I got it released with extreme difficulty and brought it back on a train.

There were many Russians still in Mongolia at various stages of repatriation. All the occupants in my apartment were Russians. I would pass them while going out or coming in, but no one appeared to be in any mood to talk. My initial impression was that I was in the midst of a people who had forgotten to smile! Possibly they were all upset, because they were being sent back to Russia and had to give up what was a comfortable living, as compared to that in Russia. Details of this I would learn from Sasha, whom I literally bumped into one day, while going up to my apartment. He immediately said, "I am sorry." At last, I had found a Russian who could speak English—in a fashion, I would later learn. Anyway, I was not going to let him go, and so, I assiduously cultivated his friendship.

Sasha was a teacher of power engineering in one of the two Technical Schools in Ulaanbaatar. He had a one bedroom apartment, very much like mine. It was fully furnished, free, and he had to pay only for food. But the prospects of going back frightened him. For instance, before coming to Mongolia, he and his pregnant wife had lived in one room in a three-story complex somewhere in Ukraine. There were rooms on either side of the hall, very much like rooms in a hotel. At the end of the hall, there was a community kitchen and a community bathroom. Three were eight rooms, four on either side. The use of the kitchen and the bathroom was strictly on a prearranged schedule. It was, of course, easy if the families got along well. In many cases, however, they did not, and as such it was a hard life.

From that kind of living, the apartment in Ulaanbaatar was like a palace, as he himself described his digs.

I used to visit Sasha and his family often. I was fond of his seven-year-old son Boris. I could trust Sasha to deal with electrical or plumbing problems in my apartment. Writing to the Ministry of Works and hoping that someone would arrive and fix the problems was a foolish dream. Occasionally, he would bring chicken, onions, and tomatoes from the Russian shop. He also introduced me to the whole new culture of wandering around in the forest and picking mushrooms.

In reality, the stint in Mongolia is replete with stories enough to fill a book. But I am limiting them to a few.

The first incident happened the day I arrived in the capital city. The plane from Moscow landed around eight in the morning. By the time I had a shower and breakfast it was close to eleven. There was no point in going to bed; also, I had an early dinner appointment with the Director of the Institute. Iglesias, the project leader, was at that time still in the Philippines.

So Enkhbat and I decided to go on a tour of the city. We had the Director's car at our disposal. The first stop was a monastery, the only one in Mongolia that was spared by Stalin. When I entered, I found a group of monks sitting on the floor of a large room, in front of low desks, in three rows filling three sides of a square. The fourth side was open at the door. There were some twenty monks.

I thought I saw the first monk lift his eyes and look at me when I entered. He was a wizened little man, with an astonishingly graceful face. I would meet him later under very strange circumstances. Devotees, not too many, entered and walked along the wall, around the square, and behind the monks. Directly opposite the door was the figure of the Buddha on a pedestal, with lamps burning at the base—a typical temple scene. When I reached that spot, I touched the feet of the deity and folded my palms together. This was almost a reflex action. When we were out of the monastery, Enkhbat asked me if I were a Buddhist. I said I was not, that I was a Hindu, and I asked him if he was a Buddhist. He said he was not either. He continued that his grandfather was, perhaps, a Buddhist. He also did not know how many people in Mongolia actually practiced Buddhism.

Many months later, he asked me, "I hear you say 'Oh, my God' occasionally. I do have a rough idea of what God means. What does it mean, what you say?"

I said that it is a cliché expressing surprise; beyond that, I did not think I could explain adequately what I meant! He left it at that.

Since this is not a travelogue, I will skip my trip to the Gobi desert, three trips to Beijing, and watching Nadam, the national celebration involving horse racing and archery, a military parade a la Russian, etc.

When Enkhbat learned about my interest in theatre and culture, he strongly urged me to see a show that was being reprised at that time—a play the title of which translates as "Crow". Apparently it had great success in the city and the regions. I was obviously curious about Mongolian theatre, and my first exposure to it was surprising, to say the least.

It was a very powerful play about social injustices and tribal loyalties, but what surprised me was that, at least three of the five women actors were completely nude on occasion. The audience seemed to take it in stride. Later, when I asked Enkhbat about it, he casually mentioned that it was nothing new, and nobody got very excited about it. It was relevant to the scene and that was that.

I also went to several music concerts, where the artists sang and played on strange-looking instruments like the nose flute. Many years later, when I heard the Silk Road Ensemble orchestrated by YoYo Ma, I felt very nostalgic.

One day, I got an interesting assignment from the office. The UNESCO had, apparently, asked that someone go to a remote community of a tribe called Tuvans. They are a nomadic herding tribe that dwells in what was considered an almost unlivable area along the Siberian-Mongolian border. The place was so isolated that one could reach there only by helicopter or by trekking through very treacherous terrain on hard saddled horses.

The concern of the UNESCO was that the Tuvans refused to leave the environs in which they lived and were inevitably marrying among themselves, in many cases cousins marrying one other, the population getting unhealthy, indeed dwindling. Was it possible to find a solution, perhaps encourage them to move to terrain that was not so remote and have access to larger towns in the country?[9]

Obviously, we had to go by helicopter. We had two interpreters with us, one of whom spoke the language of the Tuvans. From the chopper, we saw a vast expanse of green littered with white, round traditional tents called ghers (yurts). There was a narrow river flowing lazily, almost bisecting the land. Animals were grazing all over. Men and women were seen busy with their chores.

News had spread that some hot shot from the UN was coming to visit them. When the chopper landed, many people in the community, bedecked in their finest, gathered in front of the chief's yurt. After the introductions, we were invited to go inside. But first, we had to do the traditional thing—tasting aarak—which was stored at the entrance of the yurt in a large leather pouch. There was a ladle hanging from a nail on the frame of the door, which actually was a piece of canvas. The chief spooned out the booze and, having tasted it once before, I had to muster all my acting skills to pretend that I actually enjoyed the revolting stuff.

---

9   There is a fascinating video on this subject, made by John Sheppard: *The Disappearing World- The Tuvans of Mongolia.*

Once inside, we were invited to sit at a low table, which itself was built around a wood-burning stove in the middle of the yurt. There were rough-hewn stools to sit on. The chief was at the head of the table, and I was immediately to the left of him with Enkhbat beside me. A woman served on a plate a grayish mass, which looked like a chunk of meat. She set it at the center of the table. Then I was given a knife. Enkhbat told me that I should carve a piece of meat and pass the knife around. The meat looked much like a piece of steak boiled in water. Not knowing what it might taste like, I cut for myself a small piece and passed the knife around. The meat was salty with no spices of any kind. Pretty soon, the knife was back in my hand. I believe I had three or four rounds of it. This was followed by tea—black tea with a glob of butter floating on it. I was not sure if it was made with actual tea leaves or not. It was also salty in taste.

During the meal, the chief asked me many questions, observed that I did not look like a Mongolian, more like an Indian, and what I was doing in Canada, which obviously belonged to Canadians. He had met an American from the Peace Corps and didn't know what Canadians look like…

While drinking tea, Enkhbat said, "So, how do you like horse meat?" I was surprised, of course.

"Where, what horse meat?" I said, trying to hide my panic.

"Well what you ate just now is horse meat. I did not warn you because I thought you might refuse it and that would have offended the chief."

For those anxious to know what it tasted like, I recall telling myself that it was a cross between beef and moose meat.

The chief told me that the community had no desire to leave the valley. He admitted, though, that a few of the younger people had flown the coop and gone to bigger centers for making money and enjoying the "forbidden" life beyond their restricted commune. So perhaps the trip was fruitless, but for me it was an unforgettable experience.

Three months into the project, around two in the morning, I got a call from an agitated Russian woman. I did not understand anything except the word "Gabby"—the nickname of Iglesias. From her extreme agitation, I gathered that he might be sick. Then I thought that if he were just sick, Dolores, his wife, would have called me. I suspected that something serious had happened. I walked up to Enkhbat's apartment—a dangerous thing to do at that time of the night—and woke him up. I told him about the call and my suspicion. We proceeded to walk to Gabby's apartment approximately a mile away.

The same Russian woman who had called me opened the door, and when I went inside, I found Dolores lying on the sofa and sobbing uncontrollably. I realized then that Gabby was dead. He had died of a heart attack, as it turned out.

I walked into the bedroom and found him lying on his bed with his mouth and eyes open. I have to admit that I had never seen a dead body before. There have been many deaths in the family, but those happened when I was overseas. In Grande Prairie, even though I had attended several funerals, I had generally avoided "wakes" and walking past the coffin for a last look. I asked Enkhbat to close Gabby's mouth and eyes. But he refused, and so I asked the Russian woman, who reluctantly complied.

I immediately called Mr. de Mule, the Director of UNDP, and he asked me to take charge of everything and do whatever was needed to be done. The first thing to do was to inform the police. We also called the hospital for an ambulance. A van, doubling as an ambulance, arrived, but they did not have a stretcher. So I had to send the driver back to the hospital to get one. When it arrived, I noticed that it had no straps; it was just a piece of canvas stretched between two pieces of wood, very much like the army stretchers.

It took a long time before the police arrived, and they asked that the body be taken to the hospital for an autopsy. By now, it was almost six in the morning. The two policemen and the driver of the ambulance managed to put the body on the stretcher. We tied the body to the stretcher with a bed sheet.

Taking the body from the apartment to the van proved to be a very difficult task. Russian elevators are small—approximately four feet square. No one was willing to carry the body down eight floors. So we had the impossible task of trying to fit a six-foot-long stretcher with a body on it into a small elevator. The only option was to stand the stretcher and lean it against the wall, which we proceeded to do. Using a sheet to tie a dead body to a stretcher and rotate it in an elevator is something that I do not recommend. The body slid off the stretcher—half on and half out. The two policemen straightened the body, put it back on the stretcher, and held it against the wall till we reached the ground floor.

When we reached the hospital, I learned that they did not have a refrigeration system in which to store the body, until it was ready for the coffin. Also, I was told that I had to get special permission from the Chinese embassy to transport the body, because the flight from Ulaanbaatar to Manila had to pass through Beijing. The Chinese did not allow conventional coffins on board their planes. The body had to be placed in a metal casket, welded shut, and the face had to be visible through a glass window on the top panel.

Permission to transport the body was given the next day. In an insane episode, the Chinese embassy wanted a visa application, complete with a photograph. Mr. de Mule had to interfere. He had to talk to the deputy ambassador of China to get that requirement waived.

Meanwhile, I was scrambling to get a coffin made. As it turned out, the coffin, when it arrived, happened to be about four inches narrower than we needed to place the body comfortably—though I suspect it would not have made any difference to Gabby! I was anxious to seal the body in the coffin before it started decomposing. Mongolians found all this very strange. Now, the challenge was to place the body in the coffin and weld the lid on. The welder's house was about two kilometers from downtown, and he had no portable welding equipment. The body had to be taken to his house. So we went back to Gabby's house, got a shirt, suit, shoes, etc., and got a couple of staff to help me to dress the body. But Dolores insisted that a service be held before the body was sealed in the coffin. She cried and pleaded with me. I told her that there was no Catholic priest in the city, or for that matter, even a Catholic man. But she was adamant.

Yes, dear reader, your worst suspicions are going to be confirmed. Mr. de Mule could, perhaps, have done it, but he refused. There was an Anglican working for an international agency, but he was out of town. So, after a bit of tutoring from Mrs. Garcia, I did what she had asked me to do. I read the Lord's Prayer, did basic rituals as required by the widow. Then the coffin was taken to the welder's house to seal it.

Even though I am not a Christian, when I said, "Forgive us our trespasses," I genuinely meant it. I was not happy about incurring the wrath of God.

Another issue was disposing of Gabby's personal effects. He had brought a whale of a cargo with him when he arrived from Manila. This included a roll-top desk and a "sanctuary" for his private chapel! Dolores wanted to ship back much of the stuff. So boxing them and taking them to the railway station *en route* to Manila, also occupied a great deal of my time. I never received any notification that the boxes had, indeed, been delivered to Dolores. In fact, once she left Ulaanbaatar, she never got in touch with me. I thought it was a bit callous, considering the trouble I had to go through.

Oh, well!

The departure of Iglesias meant that I had to take over the administration of the project and also teach Principles of Administration or whatever the course was called. None of the students had sufficient proficiency to understand dry administrative theories. I had to speak in English, and an interpreter had to translate what I said. I had no means of finding out how accurate the translation was. But the class nodded every time they heard something, and I had to assume that I was getting to them!

The late Indian Prime Minister Rajiv Gandhi has to be credited for reintroducing Mongolia to its ancient roots. He recruited from India many scholars in Pali (a dialect that Aryans brought with them when they moved to India about 2000 years BCE), and several monks and sent them to Ulaanbaatar. In 1980, he also appointed Kushok Bakula[10], who was a highly respected Lama, as the Ambassador of India. He was also asked to travel widely to China and other countries in the Far East, where Buddhism was practiced at some time in its history, and establish a spiritual relationship with Mongolia. As such, he was a busy man, always on the go. I wanted to meet him for many reasons, and even though I requested the embassy to get me an appointment, the Ambassador was always unavailable or busy.

At the end of the first year, I had to cut short my stay in Mongolia, because my wife developed severe sciatica.

I told the First Secretary of the Indian Embassy that I could not possibly leave without seeing the Ambassador. He hastily arranged a fifteen-minute session. Not knowing what to expect—I had never been to an Ambassador's office—it was with some trepidation that I went in. I knew that he was a monk; that is all. What I saw surprised me. Here was a very large room, the floor of which was covered by a gorgeous Kashmiri rug. At one end was an enormous rosewood desk and matching chair. On it sat a small, wizened man in saffron robes, resembling very much one of the monks I had seen in the monastery twelve months before.

---

10   Kushok Bakula was born in Ladakh, India, and was a Member of Parliament. He held many high ministerial posts before he was appointed the Ambassador to Mongolia. He served in that capacity for over ten years from 1990.

He did not speak English. He did not even speak fluent Hindi! However, through our interpreters, we talked for a while. He said he knew about me from the staff and that he was aware that I had been trying to get to see him and that he was sorry, he had been busy, etc. He was also sorry to hear that I had decided to go away.

When I got up to leave, he said, "I have seen you somewhere." I did not see how, but he insisted. Then he said, "Did you by any chance come to the monastery a year or so ago?" I said I had. He was the same man I had seen on my first day, on my first and last visit to the monastery, the small man who was leading the prayers!

On the eve of my departure, I felt that the project *per se* was up and running, but the teaching part of my portfolio, except the administration courses, was not as successful as I had expected. My English students were officers in the government, and they had been working under the Russian regime, which strongly believed in hierarchy, seniority, rank, and such. The structure was what we call in administrative parlance the "line" system, as in the army.

First, I noticed that in the classroom, the first two rows in the front were reserved for the "senior" staff. A couple of weeks later, the Director of the Institute asked me whether I would be willing to hold two sessions—one for the senior administrators and another for the others. A very distinct exhibition of the class (caste?) system, I thought! I had no objection, and hence, the class was divided into two sections. Some of them wondered if I would give individual instruction, which was clearly impossible. The drop-out rate was alarming, because everyone did not perform at the same level. Some were clearly frustrated and quit.

Anyway, I think I brought a dozen of them up to a point where they could carry on a decent conversation, even though the vocabulary was not very strong. An extra year would perhaps have achieved a desirable result. Most Mongolians had their higher education in Russia, and even in Mongolia, Russian was the *lingua franca*. The use of Mongolian in schools had been banned. It was refreshing to note that, when I arrived, attempts were being made to reintroduce Mongolian in the schools. There was even a tabloid-style newspaper in Mongolian appearing once every week.

When I finally did leave, there was a very emotional farewell. To begin with, Canadians, by reputation, were popular in Mongolia, though there had not been much of a Canadian presence in the country. A Canadian of Indian origin was a novelty, and the people had a great deal of respect and affection for India, mostly as the result of the work done by the embassy. The Indian government gave many scholarships to Mongolian students to go to India for post-secondary training, especially in the field of business and agriculture.

Bidding good-bye to Sasha also turned out to be a very touching affair. The day before my departure I was invited for supper, and while enjoying a shot of vodka, I gave Boris a sealed envelope with two hundred dollar bills in it, with instructions not to open it till he reached Moscow. But he drifted into the kitchen and gave the envelope to his mother, who promptly opened it, got excited, called Sasha, and all I heard was an animated dialogue in Russian going on in the kitchen. After a while, he came out and said that he could not possibly accept it because it was a "huge" amount. I insisted. Then they both started crying. He hugged me and said that, if he exchanged the money in the black market, he would get enough rubles to buy a small piece of land in the Ukraine, because land prices were cheap, he had saved some money, and he could build his own house, have a small garden…

I promised to visit him in the Ukraine, but I have not been able to do so.

And now I am ending this on an amusing note. When I told my colleagues that I was leaving because my wife needed my presence, they were very solicitous and wanted to know what the problem was. I said that it had to do with her back and they asked me to bring her over because the Mongolians were specialists in treating back injuries. After all, for centuries they have been riding horses and falling off, all the way from Mongolia to Romania; they had to find ways of mending strained, damaged, or broken backs.

Out of curiosity, I asked them what the treatment entailed. It was very simple. The physicians have pits lined with special clay— pits deep enough for a person to stand. Once the patient is in the pit, they fill the pit with warm sand, right up to the patient's neck; but the arms will be out. The sand will then be further heated with hot coals. Once the sand reaches the optimum temperature, the physician, who would be constantly checking the pulse, (Mongolians believe that a good physician could diagnose the disease just by feeling the pulse!) would pour medicated oil on the sand, as close to the spine as possible. The treatment takes eight hours, and you come out rejuvenated, ready to ride again and, in my wife's case, sciatica free. The sand, by the way, is recycled and so I suspect it is already saturated with the oil.

I thanked them and said that it would be somewhat difficult to encourage my wife to undergo this particular procedure, however efficacious it might be.

I can't close this section without mentioning something about Genghis Khan. (Mongolians prefer *Chinggis Khaan.*) We have been led to believe that he was a monster who ruthlessly killed millions of people on his very long trek to Eastern Europe. But for the Mongolians, he was a folk hero. When I was leaving, a new hotel called Chinggis Khaan Hotel was nearing completion. A new vodka was also being brewed in Ulaanbaatar, and the company decided to call it Chinggis vodka. They defended the name with a very simple argument. If the French can name a brandy after an emperor, why not vodka named after a leader of the nation, who the Mongolians believe unified the people?

Why not, indeed!

Papua New Guinea

A few months after my return from Mongolia, I was asked to go to Papua New Guinea on a two-year assignment. This time, Nalini decided to join me. Prior research and the dossier from the UN did not necessarily paint a rosy picture of the place we were going to. It is a very diverse country with more than seven hundred native tongues. The anthropologists believe that there are as yet "undiscovered" tribes. I was also told that there are still tribes that practice cannibalism. Dangers of walking around in the dark, reports about the rash of muggings and break-ins in the capital Port Moresby, and other towns, women being treated like cattle, rape being very common, extremely venomous snakes prowling freely at night—the picture was not very encouraging! Normally, these reports would have deterred us from going. But we thought that accepting the job would give us a chance to visit Australia, New Zealand, and the South Sea Islands. It had been a dream of mine to go to the islands after reading many of Somerset Maugham's stories.

We were taking a calculated risk, but we promised ourselves that we would be careful. After all, there are thousands of expatriates in the country; one could get mugged anywhere, we argued.

Malaria was a scourge (I believe it still is), and the Health Department at the UN had warned us that common medicines, like chloroquin, were not effective and that I should get a supply of mefloquine—a new medicine on the market. We were also advised to pack a sufficient quantity of the drug, at least to last six months. After that, we could, perhaps, get them in Sydney, Australia. This medicine was reportedly the most potent; but in 1992, it was available only in the pharmacy of the University of Alberta Hospital.

I was going to leave early to get accommodation and generally settle down, and my wife was to join me after two weeks. So, I went to the hospital and procured a large jar of the grayish pills. On board the plane, I thought I would read the monograph that came with the medicine, and I was frightened out of my wits. One of the possible side-effects was epileptic attacks! When Nalini arrived, we decided to flush it down the toilet. We chose to be careful, though, taking all necessary precautions like wearing white long-sleeved shirts at night when we ventured out, sleeping under nets and so on.

The country had become independent a few years before. Rather, Australia gave up governing the country, and the people were given independence without their asking for it, much less fighting for it. The curriculum in the schools was modeled along that was used in Australia, and my job was to revise the English curriculum to reflect the culture of the country—such as it was—and teach English in the Higher Secondary School in Sogeri, a suburb of Port Moresby, the capital.

The campus had accommodation in the form of detached houses, which stood on eight foot stilts to dissuade snakes from visiting the occupants. The space under the house was graveled and served as a car porch.

Every Friday, those who did not have the luxury of their own transportation would pile into an open truck that belonged to the school and drive up to Port Moresby and return with groceries, liquor, and any other shopping to last a week. Maybe because I was older than the rest, or maybe because I was a UN staff, I was allowed to sit in front, along with the driver.

We had a large yard at the back, and so I decided to do some gardening. In addition to flowers, I grew vegetables. In a corner of the lot there was an anemic pineapple plant, which I nursed with great care. The fruit became larger day by day, and it was soon ready for harvesting. It was already turning color, and my wife asked to cut it off the plant and bring it inside. I decided to leave it for another day or two. The next day it was gone! The people believe that anything that grows in the soil belongs to everyone—first come first served. No ownership of things growing in mother earth.

The country has many betel nut palms, and the habit of chewing the nut was very prevalent. Both men and women indulged in this preoccupation, throughout the day. The nut is chewed with some lime. (Lime as in mortar; I don't mean the fruit) Obviously, a lot of saliva is produced and the lime makes it blood red in color. Since it is not good to swallow, the practice is to spit it wherever one happens to be. So it is very common to see wherever you go, blotches of red in varying stages of dryness.

The country is predominantly Christian—mostly Catholics and Seventh Day Adventists. The students were all native, and all of them were quite proficient in English. The staff was also mostly local, except one Japanese, two Australians, two Sri Lankans, two Englishmen, and me. The Japanese, Tomo Arakava, became our close friend, and we have kept in touch, albeit infrequently. The expatriates were not particularly welcome in the country; one of the reasons was the notion that they were rich. They drove cars, had fridges and other "Western" appliances, had too many clothes, and were able to buy imported liquor easily!

I can't say that the government was a properly functioning body. Sometimes it appeared that things happened in spite of the government! But I had nothing much to do with anyone except the UNDP office, and so I had no problems.

Each tribe has its own version of music and dances. The costumes, the music, and the dances are spectacular to say the least. The national bird is the "bird of paradise", with gorgeous, multicolored plumes. The tragedy was that the dancers killed the birds for their feathers to embellish their costumes.

The school had a drama program, but the teacher, Paul Kila, restricted his plays to those written in Tok Pisin. With so many tribal languages, there had to be a common language; English and Tok Pisin were the two official languages. It is actually a corrupt form of English and quite easy to learn. Try this out: *Ol kaas mus stop suppose you lukim redpla sine.* The translation appears at the end of this section.

Paul had training in theatre, and so we used to discuss matters of mutual interest. One day, Paul asked me if I would take over the rehearsal of an impending production, because he had to go to his village and would be gone for two days. I agreed, and out of curiosity, I asked him why he was going, if there was an emergency of any kind. It was an emergency of sorts, he said. Apparently his tribe was going to have a fight with a neighboring tribe, and he had to participate and defend his tribe's honor. I was aghast and I asked him if he was really serious. Sure enough, he was at war with his neighbors! Apparently, the chief of his tribe, an old man, married a young girl from the neighboring village, and he had reneged on his payment of the dowry, which was ten pigs. Pigs are very important in the daily life of the people of PNG.

I asked him how the fight was going to be carried out and what his role might be.

It was all very "civilized" according to him. The tribes would assemble in an open field early in the morning. The women from both tribes would gather and start cooking a meal for all the people. The warring males would line up facing one another, with a specified distance between them. The warriors wore cod pieces made of coconut shells or leather to protect their groins. There would be a referee to oversee the fight. On a given signal, the warring sides start shooting arrows at each other; but the aim should be below the waist. Any side did not follow this rule would lose the contest, and the other side would be declared the winner. There was some kind of complicated scoring system, which, as far as I could understand, had to do with how deep the arrow pierced the body, where it hit and so on. The referee predetermined the duration of the fight. After the set time expired, the referee would announce the winner and what the penalty for the losing side would be. The "wounded" soldiers got instant treatment, which consisted of some kind of a paste made from medicinal leaves. Scratches and such got Band-Aids. After all this, the warring factions sat down to have a feast and, of course, to get drunk, as well.

I had to ask Paul if he had done anything like this before. Yes, he had, and he showed me the scars on his thigh and calf to prove it.

Corruption in the civil service and police department was rampant. The Englishman on our staff had an interesting story to tell. He had applied for a return visa, because he wanted to go to England for a wedding. He sent the application very early, knowing how slow the response would be. Not having received any reply for a long time, he went to the office to find out the status of the application. He was prepared to bribe the person in charge. When he went there, he found out that the clerk had the application but could not locate the passport. My friend had no option but to apply for another passport, and so he got up to leave. Then he saw his passport under one of the legs of the clerk's desk. The officer had used it to stabilize his desk, which had one leg shorter than the other or, perhaps, the floor was uneven!

Our house was at the end of the paved road, which meandered a further four hundred yards or so, where there was a small store, which stocked milk, soft drinks, cookies, chocolates, bread, etc. The backyard was at the foot of a wooded hill.

The country lies over a fault line, and so, there are quakes once in a while—nothing too serious, but the ground rumbles when the quake happens. Tidal waves are also known to occur.

One day, around 2:00 a.m. on a Saturday in early December, I was awakened by some noise coming from the living/dining room. Assuming that a picture or something had fallen off the wall, I switched on the lights and proceeded to investigate the cause of the noise. My heart stopped when I saw that two guys were busy sawing off the bars of the window from outside. One of their tools had fallen into the room, which was the noise I had heard.

I was petrified, obviously. We did what we had been asked to do on occasions like this—avoid fighting, make a lot of noise, wake up the neighbors, call the police, etc. We called the police and started to make as much noise as possible, hitting pots and pans together. The neighbor, an Australian, had been at a party the previous night, and he was oblivious to what has happening! The noise frightened the culprits and they took off. It was easy to disappear into the woods. But they came back, because we could hear the gravel below crunching under their feet. We did the same thing again—making a lot of noise, hoping someone would turn up! There was no sign of the police till ten in the morning. They took a statement from us and just mentioned that they knew who the guys were. That was the end of the investigation.

Later in the day, I reported the incident to the Port Moresby office of UNDP and also the headquarters in New York. The local office immediately arranged to have a security man sleep in our house at night. It was the end of the school year, and the school was due to close for the Christmas holidays in another week or so. I submitted my resignation, because Nalini was in no mood to stay.

My suggestion that she could return to Alberta and I stay behind until I finished the contract was not acceptable!

We had leased our house in Grande Prairie for two years to someone, and so we actually had no house to return to, unless we evicted the tenants. We used the time to travel around Australia. We also traveled to New Zealand and several South Sea Islands. We stayed on what is called the Robinson Crusoe Island, where it is believed the famous man lived with his Man Friday.

While in the Solomon Islands, I committed what could be considered a crime. Guadal Canal was one of the major theatres during the Second World War, and the Allied forces had shot down many Japanese planes, which are scattered around on a vast field, now preserved as an open-air museum. Visitors could, if they wished, climb in and out of the planes, a few of which are surprisingly intact, though battered. I was sitting in the cockpit of one of the planes and fooling around with the controls when a small pipe, about six inches long, bent like a U, came apart.

I could not, of course, put it back where it was; in fact, I was not even sure where it belonged. So I took it back to Grande Prairie. I suppose I have opened myself up to all kinds of legal issues and have violated the laws of the government of the Solomon Islands. I or my estate would be happy to return it to the rightful owner, should the contingency arise.

In retrospect, we had a very interesting time in PNG. Somewhat unsettling, but interesting, nonetheless. I got reasonably proficient in Tok Pisin, but today I am afraid I have lost it all. I am sure it will all come back to me if I visit the country and stay there for a couple of weeks. The same thing could be said about Mongolian, too.

Something else that I think is important to mention here is that, though it was a backward country, all the houses, including public institutions, had solar panels on the roof for heating water!

p.s. Translation of the sentence in Tok Pisin: All cars must stop if you see a red sign.

Cambodia

The next assignment offered to me was to Cambodia to a city called Siem Reap, very close to Anghor Wat. It was an interesting assignment: to start a teachers training college from scratch. But the place was still considered dangerous, because there were land mines all over the place, and nobody knew exactly where they were. Also, the contract said that electricity would be available for only four hours every day, but kerosene would be available in plenty!

I had to decline. Also I realized that many of the UNDP assignments were to unstable or under-developed countries, with known and unknown challenges and, hence, I asked to be removed from the roster.

I decided to run for public office as a trustee in the Public School District. I served the Board for the mandatory three years. I am sure I could have gotten myself reelected, but I chose not to, because I realized after the first term that I was not cut out to be a politician.

At the end of my term, I joined the Canadian Executive Services Organization (CESO).

CESO-Canadian Executive Services Organization

Russia

The UNDP, the UN's global development network, chiefly connects countries to knowledge, experience, and resources to help people build a better life. Every country in the world, including The Republic of Cape Verde (population 500,000) has an office. In any given month, there will be experts in nearly a hundred countries, working with the people to find their own solutions to global and national development challenges.

But the needs of the developing countries have been too enormous, and the demands on the UNDP too overwhelming, so that the organization had been forced to farm out the requests to many countries that have the resources to provide help—especially in projects that require short-term involvement.

The Canadian Executive Services Organization in Canada (CESO), the Volunteer Services Organization (VSO) in England, and the Australian Volunteers International (AVI) are three examples of organizations that provide assistance to developing countries throughout the world. They draw from an almost inexhaustible pool of experts in all possible fields of human endeavor.

Most of the CESO assignments are less than a month in duration. But, to me, the most important thing was that whenever I traveled, I could collect Aeroplan (frequent traveler) points! Also, the short duration of the assignment suited me more, considering that I was growing mentally unprepared for long absences from home.

My first assignment was in 2000 to Izhevsk, Russia. I was seventy two years old at that time. I was asked to evaluate the English curriculum at the Udmurtia State University, give workshops for teachers, and evaluate their performance in the classroom. The project was for three weeks.

But getting to Izhevsk was itself an interesting experience. The first eye opener was the airport in Moscow. The arrival lounge was too small to accommodate two or three hundred passengers. (I am not sure if that space has been enlarged since my last visit.) Though I was allowed to go through the VIP immigration desk, many people were thronged there, too. You could become an instant VIP if you slipped a ten-dollar bill in your passport. Others struggled at the remaining five or six counters, where there was nothing like a queue. Strength prevailed.

Once out of the immigration area, I went to collect my baggage. I had two rather heavy bags, one of which contained mostly books. I was prepared, not knowing what kind of reference materials would be available in the University library. (Nothing much, as it turned out.) So I needed a cart, since one of my bags did not have wheels; and strangely enough, I could not find any. Rather, attached to each of the few carts available, was a Russian, complete with moustache, woolen cap, and a serious face. In other words, I had to pay them to get the use of the cart.

I had no choice, of course. But once outside, Alexander Sergeev of the Russia desk was waiting for me, and he negotiated the price. I was put up in a hotel very close to the Kremlin. In fact, I could see the famous onion-shaped domes of St.Basil's Cathedral from my room.

The next day, I flew to Izhevsk and was met by my interpreter Razalia Gainullina. She is a Tatar.[11] Everyone called her Rose.

Izhevsk is the capital of the Udmurt Republic of Russia. Most of the people are Muslims. During the Soviet days, it was established as a place where all manner of metalworking was done, especially in the manufacture of machinery and arms. One of the most famous weapons, the AK 47, was designed by a local man called Mikhail Kalashnikov, and was manufactured in a factory very close to the university. Until the fall of the Soviet Union, it was a closed city with no access to foreign people. Eventually, many of the armament factories were shut down, throwing thousands of people out of work, and resulting in serious unemployment, alcoholism, broken homes, and divorces.

Chayikovsky, named after the great composer Tchaikovsky, is about two hours from Izhevsk by car. The famous composer was

---

11   Tatars, sometimes spelled Tartars, are a Turkic ethnic group living in Turkey, Uzbekistan, Kazakhstan, Ukraine, Tajikistan, Kyrgyzstan, Turkmenistan, Azerbaijan and, of course, Mongolia.

born in a place called Votkinsk, a few miles south of the city. The house in which he grew up is maintained as a museum. Needless to say, I visited the town and the museum. During that particular time, the building was being renovated outside and inside. Outside, on the scaffolding, I saw seven painters wearing coveralls. They were all women! I noticed this in the university as well. On the faculty there was, perhaps, one man for every ten women. This is a problem that is causing concern all over Russia because, demographically, there are more women than men in that country.

Though there are many stories to tell, I will restrict myself to two, because both affected me deeply.

Anton Denisovitch, one of the professors at the university, once asked me if I would be kind enough to visit his parents in their dacha outside the city. His parents had never seen a foreigner, and he wondered if I would be willing to join the family for supper! I said I was as foreign as anyone he could possibly get! I said, also, that I would be delighted to meet his parents.

It was arranged that we would go early, relax in the banya (sauna) for half an hour or so, and have an early supper. On the way, I told Anton that I would like to stop by and get a bottle of vodka. He said there was no need, because all that had been taken care of. In that case, I said that I would like to get some flowers for his mother. He agreed and, after a while, stopped the car by the roadside, where I found a woman with a few flowers on a newspaper in front of her.

What usually happens is this. The poor women in the city go to cemeteries, weddings, wedding receptions, etc., collect whatever flowers are available, open up a "stall" on the wayside and hope to make a few rubles. I could not help laughing, and I told him that I must go to a proper florist. The shop was a bit out of the way, but he agreed. There, I got a dozen roses. (Selling scrounged flowers is not by any means unique to Russia. French Gypsies called Romas—refugees from Romania and Bulgaria—routinely sold them in front of temporary shelters on A86 Highway circling Paris. Since I started writing this, the French government had started deporting them to their countries of origin.)

His parents were eagerly waiting for me. Both were dressed semi-formally, and when I gave the flowers to Anton's mother, she broke out in tears and said that, in all her life, nobody ever had given her flowers. She had not even *seen* a bunch of a dozen roses! Obviously, it was a very emotional scene.

Anton played the role of interpreter, the conversation mostly on how the "others" lived. Did I have a TV? Did I live in a house or in an apartment? What kind of a car did I drive? Did all Canadians get medical assistance from the government, and how much did it cost? Is the army powerful? What do the Canadians think of Russians? Questions—hundreds of them—mostly out of a giant curiosity about the outside world.

Mrs. Denisovitch wanted to know if I had by any chance a picture of my family. I produced one from my wallet, and she declared that I had a beautiful family.

As I mentioned earlier, Mr. Danisovitch had not had seen a foreigner, nor had he been outside Russia! The only trips he had ever made were to Moscow and that, too, on official business. He was a top-ranking civilian officer in the army in charge of managing the munitions factory, which apparently he had run very efficiently, enough for the government to take note. For his services, he was presented with a medal of honor—more like a lapel pin—something that was given only to very select officers outside the army.

We had a marvelous time. The men spent close to an hour in the banya. (You take a cold shower every fifteen minutes or so.) The meal was sumptuous to say the least. Mother had prepared Russian specialties for the "foreigner".

When I was ready to leave, Mr. Denisovitch said that he had been honored by my visit and that, as a token of appreciation, I should have something from the family, and he gave me the pin that had been a topic of discussion earlier. I said that I could not possibly accept something so valuable, but he insisted. Arguably, that pin is one of the most valuable things that I have collected over the many years I have been tramping around the world.

I shall also never forget the scene when I took my leave—Mr. Denisovitch holding me in a bear hug, a gentler hug from his teary-eyed wife. And, of course, the customary kisses!

Rose, my interpreter, was a divorced woman living with her preteen daughter. Her parents were in another apartment nearby. Rose had blonde hair, or so I thought. One day, I noticed tell-tale signs that she had dyed her hair. I told her that I was in the theatre business and could recognize tinted hair when I saw it. She admitted that she had.

"What was the original color?" I asked.

"I was a brunette," she said.

Then she went on to say why she had decided to color her hair. Her younger brother had finished his matriculation, and it was mandatory that all high school graduates serve two years in the army. After training for six months, he was sent to Afghanistan. Two months later, she got a letter from the army to say that her brother had been killed. I believe she got the notification around five in the afternoon. The next day, more than half of her hair had turned gray. In another day, she was completely gray, and so she decided to dye her hair. (For proof that stress can turn a person's hair gray, just look at the before and after pictures of Barack Obama!)

She said that her parents had not yet recovered from the shock. Her father developed heart problems, and her mother stopped talking, unless it was absolutely necessary.

Her husband became an alcoholic when the armament factory was closed. He had no skill in any other field. She had no job, and the situation became too difficult to manage. After the divorce, she went back to university where she completed her degree in English, and the President gave her a job as a teaching assistant. When I met her, she had a full-time job as a lecturer. She was an excellent teacher, and a great interpreter.

I was sent two more times to Izhevsk, in 2001 and 2004 on different assignments. I must admit, though, that I have lost touch with my friends, including Rose. I used to send her books. I also had noticed that she had only one dress and two coats—a fall coat and a winter coat! So I used to send her material for making dresses for herself and her daughter. (Her mother was an accomplished seamstress.)

❧

My second assignment in Russia was in 2000 as well. This time, I was sent to Zlatoust to help establish an English Centre. There was already a centre of sorts, meaning that a few students used to meet in a house where two teachers gave instruction. The students met after regular school hours and during weekends. But the manager wanted to set it up as a proper school, with policies, an attractive curriculum, a publicity protocol, pay scales, fee schedules, etc. It was a private enterprise, and hence, there was no interference from the government and bureaucrats.

When I first went there, the school had sixty students. The manager, Elena Alekseyvana Urventseva, was a smart go-getter, but she did not have the clout in the city to attract supporters. Also, a woman could not get anywhere in the business world in Russia; it was male territory. So, one of the things I could do, in addition to helping the teachers, was to use my gravitas—my status as Officer of the UN and as a representative of the Government of Canada—to open doors. I had meetings with the Mayor and the city council, the President and the English faculty of the University, the Chamber of Commerce, the leaders of the Arts community (Zlatoust has a great professional theatre company), and the members of the medical profession. I talked to leading businessmen and bankers.

I went to Zlatoust again, I believe, in 2004, and the school had grown considerably. They were operating in three buildings instead of one.

On 18 December 2010, the Centre celebrated its tenth anniversary. Elena told me that she had six hundred students, and the number could only increase. She wanted to thank me in a big way. She mentioned how I was solely responsible for the growth of the school and asked if I could possibly attend the function. In an insane moment, I thought I might take the trip. But health issues sobered me, and I had to accept kudos through cyberspace! However, I prepared a video with my message, which, apparently, Elena played before a tuxedo/long-gown gala audience.

Early in September of 2001, I was sent to a city called Vladimir, which has a very large Jewish community. The Jewish Cultural Centre in Vladimir is called Hesed Lev, and they got a grant from the UNESCO in response to their request for funds to promote Jewish culture through the performing arts. Many Jews had been killed during the Soviet regime, and the younger generation was growing up without any knowledge of or sensitivity to their rich heritage. Hesed Lev wanted to tour the country, especially the Baltic States, with a tight production of plays, dances, folk songs, etc. The grant from the UNESCO would underwrite their expenses, but they wanted someone to put a show together and organize a "Festival", which could be taken on the road.

It was a very exciting project. The original intention was to open the festival in Moscow and start touring after that.

The center had arranged my accommodation with one of the staff, a young Jewish volunteer named Katrina, and a few days after my arrival, she told me that her grandfather, Dr. Dubov, would like to meet me and would I be kind enough to join him and his wife for dinner? His parents had been political prisoners during the Soviet regime.

"Would he care to talk about it?" I asked Katrina.

Normally he did not like to, but she was sure he would make an exception. I told her to warn him that I just might pry.

Dr. Dubov received me at the door. The first thing I noticed was his astonishing resemblance to actor Rex Harrison!

The deep furrows on a prematurely aged face bore eloquent testimony to a life of pain, harsh memories, trauma, and anger. The tall frame was gaunt, the gait slow, but dignified. The brown eyes had a fierce glint.

Prof. Roid Dubov—PhD in Geophysics, D.Sc in Geological Chemistry—was one of the most respected scientists in Russia. He was also an internationally known geologist. He had retired as Chair of Geology at the Vladimir Polytechnic University. He spoke English in a fashion and, when stuck for the appropriate word, daughter Aksana would come to his rescue. Aksana was a professor of English at the University. His wife, Susanna Dubov, had a typical Russian supper laid out in the living room. Meals were usually eaten in the kitchen.

"My English is not very good. No chance to practice. But if you stay with me for a month, it will come back to me," Dubov said with a chuckle. "But Aksana helps."

"You are doing all right," I encouraged him.

"I have been to Canada. Very friendly people. The Rockies fascinated me. Banff is so beautiful. We don't have anything like that in Russia. I was the keynote speaker at an international conference of geologists. This was in Ottawa, twenty-five years or so ago. Of course, I had an interpreter."

He excused himself and brought a bound edition of the proceedings of the conference. He showed me his contribution. Twenty-five years ago, he looked strikingly handsome. But the furrows were still there and also the fiery look in his eyes.

Quite understandable, as it turned out.

When you are six years old, if twelve soldiers wielding machine guns arrest your father before your very eyes, the incident is bound to leave an indelible scar. A few days later, the soldiers came for his mother. He had clear memories of the day… how his mother cried, how the soldiers roughed her up. A few months later, he would learn that his father had been executed. His mother was not killed, only because she was a robust, good-looking woman.

"I was offered a job by the Canadian government," he said. "But I chose to return to Russia. This is my homeland."

A cloud passed over his face, and after a brief moment of introspection, he added, "Yes. This is home, whatever happened."

"But you have bitter memories," I prompted. I had been wondering all along how to broach the subject.

"Yes, I do," he said.

"But what crimes did your parents commit? What were they accused of?" I asked.

"That was bizarre," he said with some help from Aksana for the word "bizarre". "My father was the chief engineer of South-eastern Railways."

It turned out Dr. Dubov's father was a high-ranking officer. His deputy was jealous of him and had an eye on the job. Knowing that his boss would be at the helm of affairs for a long time, he regularly fed stories to the party officials saying that Dr. Dubov was not a Bolshevik and had clear anti-communist views. This must have gone on for many months. Anyway, as I mentioned earlier, both his parents were arrested. No reasons were given.

Apparently, they were sent to different camps in Siberia. After ten years, his mother was transferred to another camp, because she had already contracted gonorrhea. During the transfer, when the train was approaching a town, she managed to let fly out of the train a letter with details about where she had been and where she was going.

Dr. Dubov continued his story. "It was a miracle that someone picked up that letter and took it to my grandfather. I grew up with my grandfather. I was sixteen when I saw my mother again."

There was no emotion when he described the scene.

"I had always remembered her as a very beautiful woman, somewhat chubby, with large, piercing eyes. But the person standing before me was a gaunt, skinny woman. Her bones were sticking out. She was almost bald. The large blue eyes were in two sunken holes on the face. At first, I was not prepared to accept that she was my mother. Then she said, 'Roey!' And I burst out crying. I cried for many days. She died two years later."

His eyes wandered again…painful images.

Then it was time for toasts. The first of many was a welcome to the Canadian guest and the second to peace in the world.

Four days later, the World Trade Center was destroyed!

"Do you feel uncomfortable talking about those days?" I asked.

"It was difficult in the beginning. Now I don't mind. In any event, I talk about this only to special people. You are special. It is a great thing you are doing. Hesed Lev is doing a great job, trying to promote Jewish culture and Jewish tradition. One does not realize how easy it is to destroy and how difficult to rebuild. The Soviets broke the backbone of the Russian Jews."

The meal, as usual, was great. It was time for good-byes.

"It has been an honor," he said. "I wish I could speak better English. Will you come again?"

"I'll try," I said.

But I did not go again, due to pressure of work and because of an *insane* event that rocked the whole world. What remains of that visit now is a memory—memories of atrocities committed against humanity, memory of a man who lived with deep scars and with a feeling of outrage and helplessness, a man who immersed himself in academic pursuits to forget his pain, forget memories of how a respectable Jewish family was devastated, destroyed, ravaged.

Vladimir also had (still has, I presume) the most notorious prison in the whole country, so much so that the hardened criminals or those who needed to be "taught a lesson" were sent to Vladimir.

On the 6th of September, I got a strange call from the Russia desk in Moscow. They had a request from the UNESCO office. Three Israelis would be arriving in Vladimir on the 9th. They were journalists who wrote articles of protest against the Russian occupation of the erstwhile Czechoslovakia. At that time, they were operating independently from Moscow, Odessa, and Kiev for different news organizations. They were arrested at the same time and sent to Vladimir state prison.

On their discharge after six years or so, they decided to move to Israel. They were returning to Vladimir after many years to visit the prison, where they had been incarcerated, where they withstood indescribable torture, but survived simply because of their indomitable spirit.

So the call was a request to interview them and submit a report. I arranged for them to meet me on the 11th of September.

The plight of the journalists at the hands of the prison authorities and the torment they went through are not relevant to this memoir. But to listen to these three people describe their experiences, coming just a few days after listening to Dr. Dubov's tragic story was a bit too much to take. I had to ask them why, in heaven's name, they came back to Vladimir. They said that they wanted to see once more the place where they fought the brutal machinery of the KGB and beat it. They were involved in writing a book, describing their experiences, and they wanted to brush up on a few details, mostly details about the city itself, which they had not had an opportunity of seeing, having spent all the time in the prison.

It turned out to be a very disturbing day.

I came home around 5:00 p.m. Dinner was not until after six. Katrina had to come and prepare it. Normally, I don't watch Russian television. First, I don't have sufficient command of the language to understand the content. I could manage small talk, basic shopping and such, but could not follow serious dialogue or newscasters. The TV regularly showed English movies dubbed in Russian. Somehow, Clint Eastwood saying, "Go ahead, make my day," did not sound authentic when spoken in Russian!

Anyway, I got myself a cold beer and turned the television on just to divert my troubled mind, and I saw this strange image of a plane crashing into the Twin Towers. There was a commentary going on, but I did not understand it, except the words "New York". There was also the scroll at the bottom, but I could not understand that, either. I thought that James Cameron or Steven Spielberg was filming some sort of movie involving the towers!

In about ten minutes, Katrina called to say that she would be a bit late because they were watching TV and that I should turn it on if I had not done so. I said I had but did not know what it was all about. Then she told me what exactly was happening. I sat watching for while, could not take it anymore, and turned off the television. Of course, I had no details about the perpetrators, the reason for this destruction, the extent of the damage, etc.

After the initial shock, I was overwhelmed by a personal outrage. During my many months spent in New York, sometimes I would to go to the Towers. The North Tower had a restaurant complex called Windows on the World on the 106th and 107th floors. The restaurant had strict dress codes and was extremely pricey. But it also had a bar called "The Greatest Bar on Earth", which was more casual and affordable. The view from the bar was spectacular. Looking out through the full-length windows, one could see the southern tip of Manhattan, where the Hudson and East Rivers met. One could also see the Liberty State Park and Staten Island, with the Verrazano-Narrows Bridge.

I recalled how my dear friend and former boss, Dr. Henry Anderson, and I spent a whole afternoon there, discussing, among other things, Plato and the qualities of the ideal administrator and how the Greek could have been of great help if he were alive in the twentieth century!

I felt personally violated.

When Katrina came home, she had a message from the Director of Hesed Lev. She strongly advised me to shave off my beard. The TV was showing hazy photographs of suspected criminals, and I looked like one of them!

I did not, of course, heed her advice.

The next day, I was asked to pack up and leave for Canada. I was asked to take the train to Moscow instead of flying. From Moscow, I was taken to an undisclosed place, and put on a plane the next day. I recall that it was a very circuitous route by which I reached Edmonton. Needless to say, I could not stay until the contract was finished. I don't know how successful the festival was, but I do know that they did not open in Moscow.

Anyone who goes to Russia makes it a point to go to St Petersburg, and I was no exception. I believe I visited the city after a brief assignment in Kazan. Sergeev had arranged for someone to meet me at the railway station. I did all the mandatory touristy things: Peterhof, The Hermitage, dining by the canals, The Kirov Ballet...

One afternoon, I was being driven around the city when a policeman stopped the car. He asked my escort for something. In response, she opened her purse and gave him 100 rubles, and we were on our way. I was, of course, curious about what had happened. She said that he wanted to see a certain document that she did not have in the car, but she could produce it later, for which she would have to go to the police station, and she did not know how long she would have to wait in the station before she was cleared of any misdemeanor. It was much easier to give him his bribe and get on with life! She also said that this was a very common occurrence, and normally, she would have gone to the police station, but since I, a foreigner, was in the car, the police could get more difficult just to impress me. I offered to reimburse her but she smiled it off.

Any account of my experiences in Russia would be incomplete without a mention of the privilege I had of meeting Constantin Skvortsov. I first met him in 2001. Some people consider him the Shakespeare of Russia. He is a great playwright and an artist, specializing in woodcuts. He lived in the Artists' Colony just outside Moscow. One of the memorable experiences was going with him to visit Boris Pasternak's grave. Pasternak had lived a mere five houses from Skvortsov.

When I met him, one of his plays called *George* was being translated into English by a friend of his. Apparently, it had tremendous success across the country, and he desperately wanted it presented to the English-speaking world. He asked if I would look at the translation when it was finished and, knowing my interest in theatre, if I would produce it somewhere. I agreed to do what I could.

In 2002, I saw Skvortsov again. The translation was ready, and I brought it with me and went through it carefully. But I thought it did not read well. It certainly was not stage worthy as it was written. The translator could not capture the passion of the play. Mind you, I only have secondhand reports about the import and power of the original. I was forthright and told him that the translation lacked power, and it needed further work.

I first went to Russia in 2000; the last trip was in 2004. In between, I believe I went six times. The changes I had seen in the five years were astonishing. It appeared that construction of new high-rises was going on constantly. During the second visit, driving from the airport, I was surprised to see the familiar Ikea sign! The next year, I saw BMW and Mercedes dealerships. In 2004, I saw a Jaguar and Rolls Royce/Bentley dealership. In 2004, I was staying in a high-end hotel in Moscow and there in the foyer were pamphlets from real estate agents. Out of curiosity, I picked up one. It had listings of houses for rent or purchase. Some of the rental properties went for $18000 American dollars a month!

I suppose there is nothing much to feel surprised about. After all, if Aurel Braun of the University of Toronto is to be believed, (c.f. *Toronto Globe and Mail*, September 29, 2010) Moscow has the second largest number of billionaires in the world.

When I was in Izhevsk for the first time, Rose, my interpreter, got a monthly salary of 600 rubles a month; and a dollar was worth 10 rubles. Today, as I write this, a dollar is worth 30 rubles. Do some arithmetic. How much should a person have to earn to be able to afford a rental apartment for $18,000 a month?

The Philippines

In 2004, I was also sent to the Philippines. This was soon after I had returned from Zlatoust. The assignment was to develop the English and Drama program in a private Montessori school. A billionaire owned the school. The Principal, the wife of the owner, was a trained pediatrician but she chose to go into education.

The school is situated in Tarlac City. This place is famous as the hometown of the Aquinos. They are the richest family in Tarlac; in fact, I believe, they own the Hacienda Luisita Golf Course—an eighteen-hole piece of real estate that I think would rival many of the golf courses in the world.

It is always the responsibility of the client to provide accommodation and food for the consultants. The CESO representative met me at the airport in Manila, and we were on our way to Tarlac City some three hours away from Manila. Among other things, he said I would be staying at the Asiaten Rest House. I was a bit miffed. I wanted either an apartment with all the amenities or a decent hotel, but a rest house? I did not know that the owner of the rest house was the billionaire owner of the school!

The "rest house" turned out to be a big surprise. It was attached to his house, and it had several rooms. The facility was meant to accommodate his friends and high-placed officials and politicians who often came from Manila to Tarlac City to play golf. There was a restaurant attached to the facility, and the food for the family and visitors was prepared in the restaurant.

I must say that I had never met a billionaire before, (I know a few millionaires, but the b's? No!) and I had no idea how they lived! The house was itself very large with a spacious courtyard. At any given time, there were at least three cars parked there.

I was given a suite with an office and bedroom. There was a kitchenette, just in case I chose to make a cup of tea or fry an egg or make a toast after the restaurant was closed at 10.00 p.m. The fridge was loaded with stuff. There was a fruit basket on the table, which would be replenished every day. There was a mini bar, and several bottles of wine and beer in the fridge. If I opened a bottle of beer, it would be replaced, as soon as I left for work.

Needless to say, I was treated royally. My host was a "business-man", though I had no idea what business he was in. I came to learn later that he was very close to the Marcos family, about whom he spoke very highly.

Manila is like many American cities—huge shopping malls, boutiques, fancy restaurants, and what not. There are so many rich people there, it is truly astonishing. And yet, there are many more people living in poverty. Several people I got acquainted with also would share their one ambition and hope—to immigrate to Canada. One of the teachers in the school told me that she would be willing to work as a nanny for me for $400 a month!! The school was an elitist institution, well equipped, the students obviously from wealthy families, handsomely dressed in uniforms. But I had no idea how much the teachers were paid; I never asked. One has to assume that they were paid much more than those in the public system.

I had a very enjoyable three weeks there. My host took me to the various clubs, casinos, and the ritzy restaurants. Every weekend, we made a trip to Manila with the family. Since we were literally living in the same house, I was treated as part of the family. Sometimes, we had our meals together. They loaded me with gifts. I was truly sorry to leave them. However, I must add that I have lost all contact with them, though during our last supper, they did promise to keep in touch.

The day before I was due to leave Tarlac City for Manila, we got reports that a band of rebel soldiers had commandeered a helicopter, gone to the international airport, hovered around the control tower, and shot dead all the staff in the tower. Naturally, I could not leave until I got clearance from the Canadian Embassy. The army had to coax the rebels back to *terra firma*, and once they landed, they were arrested and jailed for life.

By now my health was getting erratic. I had already been diagnosed with diabetes a few years before. I had to have an angiogram done and a stent was inserted into the coronary artery; the doctors also diagnosed that I have unstable angina. Traveling was becoming difficult and tiresome, and so I decided not to accept any more international assignments.

Also in July of 2005, I had a near-death experience back in Grande Prairie. Even though I already had a stent, I continued to get discomfort in the chest. Once it got too severe and, fearing that the stent might have been displaced, I went to the hospital. To ensure that the stent, indeed, had not been displaced, I was sent for an angiogram. All major cardiac issues are dealt with in Edmonton, 320 miles away. I was taken in an air ambulance.

For those who don't know the insides of this vehicle, let me just say that it is a very crowded space! Two paramedics, surrounded by tubes, scopes, dials, and various life-support systems manage to sit around a "bed", which is not substantially wider or longer than an ironing board! The patient is zippered up in a body bag; the only option is whether you want your arms out or inside the bag. Straps at three strategic locations secure the body.

Anyway, in Edmonton, the angiogram did not reveal anything wrong. (Let me say, though, that to come to this conclusion, they had to insert a tube in my femoral artery, right up to the heart.) Probably gastric reflux caused the discomfort, the doctor suggested. He changed my medication a bit and sent me home.

Earlier that day, the meteorologist had issued warnings that there was a good chance for thunderstorms later that afternoon. But all the same, the pilot decided to fly back to Grande Prairie.

About fifteen minutes before landing, the weather did turn ugly, as forecast, and the small aircraft started pitching and heaving. Unbeknownst to the paramedics, who had been carefully monitoring my pulse, etc., the wound in the groin had opened up, resulting in serious bleeding. But no one knew about it. I told them that I did not feel well, and they mistook that I was nauseated and so they injected gravol into the IV. I complained again and one of the paramedics, on a hunch I am sure, unzipped the bag. She let out a scream! I was soaking in blood. My daughter was accompanying me, having secured a seat where the co-pilot usually sits. I don't need to tell what she was going through! The paramedic put both hands on the wound and applied as much pressure as she could. Another kept on asking me questions for which answers were obvious, ostensibly to confirm that I was still lucid. I said that I was going to throw up. They did provide a container to collect the stuff, but I don't think it helped much, when I eventually threw up. I do not recommend that you do this while lying on your back! Half of the stuff came out, and I choked on the other half of my vomit.

I recall that everything blacked out, but I also felt that I was surrounded by a strange light or warmth.

It is said that, just before death your entire life passes before your eyes…in your consciousness, I guess. Well, I can vouch for it. Your life does pass by in a flash, much like what you would experience if you took a paperback and fanned the pages from the end of the book to the beginning. The pages of your life flutter by, very fast.

My consciousness, or whatever, was filled with images of my past life, flying past, as I said, at a furious speed. Strangely enough, I also experienced an overwhelming sense of fragrance and color, with the heads of my parents popping in and out, competing with scenes from the past. My family figured, as well, in the magic lantern show of the mind!

When I regained consciousness, I was in the intensive care unit.

With such potential problems a possibility, and not wanting to go through such nightmares in a foreign country, I decided that it was better to stay closer to home.

However, I just *had* to undertake two more pleasure trips, bad health notwithstanding.

One was to cross the Panama Canal. I believe I was ten years old when my teacher tried, fruitlessly I might add, to explain the intricate system of locks. Somehow, it did not make sense; I did not understand how it could possibly be done. At that age, you knew that the lock is something that you opened with a key. I had read up on the engineering feat, later, while I was in college, but I had to see it actually work. So Nalini and I took a cruise from Fort Lauderdale in Florida, crossed the canal, and went on to Los Angeles. The lock system is something to behold—especially considering that it was built in 1914.

I had to take one more trip to Wimbledon, the cathedral of tennis. This was not the first trip to Wimbledon. I took in a lot of tennis while I was a student in London. A few years ago, I went with my son Nikku, as part of an ambitious project to see all grand slams in tennis. This time, I went with my daughter Radha, knowing that it would be the last visit. As could be expected we had several hours of rain and a few hours of tennis!

We also took that opportunity to go to Iceland to see the midnight sun. Of course, I could have seen it in Canada, but somehow I thought Iceland would be more exotic! We stood outside our hotel in Reykjavik at midnight; we felt as if it was 9 p.m. on a summer's evening in Grande Prairie. Iceland would also be the forty-first country I had been to, for one reason or another.

CHAPTER SIX

HELPING HANDS

Hindus by and large are fatalists. *Que sera, sera!*

When I was growing up, I used to see several mendicants (one could say beggars, I suppose) turning up occasionally around noon asking for something to eat. Many of them wore saffron robes. They were not monks per se, but having renounced everything they wandered around praying in temples and seeking alms. In the evening they slept on the floor of any temple they were close to. They talked little, and some of them had expert knowledge in the use of medicinal herbs. Some of them also appeared to have the power of divination, as it turned out.

I believe I was fourteen or so when one of these men came to our house. I recall it was during the summer school break. As usual, mother gave him food, which he ate sitting under the mango tree in the yard. My brother and I were watching him from a corner. When he was done, he went up to the well, drew water, and cleaned the plates. While setting the plates on the verandah, he saw us. He pointed at me and said I would do a lot of traveling when I grew up and spend most of my life away from home. He looked at my brother and asked him his date of birth. He appeared to make some mental calculation of sorts and told my brother that certain planets are "aspecting" unfavorably and, thus, his life would be shorter than mine—perhaps a politically incorrect thing to say! My mother overheard this and got furious and asked the man never to come to the house again.

My brother died six years ago when he was seventy. And I, well! The above narrative appears to have vindicated the man!

Deep down, I was consumed with the desire to go away from the immediate environment in which I was living. It was perhaps a subliminal thing, due to the dissatisfaction and confusion I grew up with. Perhaps I was living the clichéd phrase "distant pastures are greener". But having a fairly scientific bent of mind, I was not about to believe the mendicant, whose prophesy I dismissed with some contempt. Sometimes, when I am in a pensive mood and reflecting on the early days, I cannot but believe that it was sheer luck or accident that I chanced upon the advertisement by the British government. Was it fate? Do I ascribe to fate all that has happened to me? Was it all destined to happen? Did I have to play no role at all?

I think not. Even if fate or luck or whatever might have shaped my destiny, I have to admit that I needed to work very hard and perhaps help "fate" along a little! But I also know that sheer hard work alone would not have put me where I am. For my advancement or accomplishments—however small—I had the support of many people during the crucial stages of my life and career. I also had the privilege of meeting or listening to some of the most exciting and inspiring people. I want to devote this chapter to a few who were close to me, who have helped me, who have influenced me, whom I have admired. These people shaped my thinking, molded my character, encouraged me to go ahead, or gave a helping hand. This list is by no means exhaustive. There are many others who deserve to be mentioned, but considerations of space have constrained me to limit the number.

My parents

<u>Mr. Parameswaran Nair and Mrs. Jagadamma</u>

I want to say the following to complement what I have already mentioned about my parents. My father and his brother lost their mother when they were very young and were brought up by their aunt—their mother's sister. My grandfather was a Namboothiri from the north, and grandmother was a Nair. In those days, Namboothiris—a step higher than Brahmins—never married outside the caste. I imagine this is still true in some parts of Kerala. So I must say that I am a bit intrigued by this relationship. Possibly, she was married to one of the younger members of the clan. Anyway, it appears that his wife died when the kids were very young, and he promptly abandoned them, leaving them in the care of his wife's sister. They were six and four years old at that time. So it was the aunt who brought up my father and uncle.

My father's aunt, whom we called "ammachi", had three daughters and a son. I have no recollection of seeing her husband. All I remember is that the house was very large and that father's cousins and their children grew up together. It was a very large, extended family. The house was in the middle of the city and had no yard to speak of, neither in the front nor the back.

I have very distinct memories of ammachi as I write this. What I recall about her, and indeed her daughters, is that they were always dressed in the traditional Nair garb—a two-piece ensemble. They did not wear blouses and, hence, their shoulders were bare. They also wore enormous earrings, which filled a hole on the lobe. When the earrings were removed, one could see a huge loop at the bottom of the ear. I vividly recall my daughter, when she was three years or so, sitting on the lap of one of my aunts and playing with this loop! I believe my aunts "modernized" their attire in the early forties, but ammachi always wore the traditional dress.

My father did not appear to have inherited any wealth from his father. His aunt, herself a widow, was in charge of the domestic staff in the Maharaja's (King) palace and wielded a great deal of influence. She put my father through university. My uncle did not go beyond middle school. But he became a reasonably successful farmer.

Namboothiris were famous for their scholarship, love of the arts, music, and such, and it appears that my father inherited many of these qualities. He was a great lover of nature. I had always suspected that he did not have a sense of humor. I have never heard him tell a humorous story. He enjoyed comedy, though; I remember him lustily laughing at some of the comedies in which I had appeared. I am sure I desperately sought his nod of approval. He attended all the plays I was in and would give terse compliments about my performance. Though he was a director in his own right, he never offered any suggestions; that is the job of the director, he must have told himself.

In the capital city, Thiruvananthapuram, we have what is called "The Museum". Obviously, the complex has a museum that exhibits many artifacts, especially relating to the rich heritage of Kerala. There is also a zoo and the many acres on which the zoo is situated are also preserved as a botanical garden. Every tree and shrub is labeled with its generic and specific names. Tucked away in an idyllic corner, there is also a small art gallery called "Chitralayam".

The surroundings of the museum are a horticulturist's delight. The well-manicured lawns had several hundred flowerbeds, which had a bewildering variety of roses and other flowering plants. Obviously, they had their own nursery, the manager of which was a distant cousin of my father. I believe that was the source of the roses and other plants we had in our garden.

I remember when I was a small boy, my father occasionally used to take me to the complex and let me wander around, especially in the museum and the art gallery. I was probably eight or ten years old. But my father's cousin would ensure that someone escorted me wherever I went. The art gallery fascinated me. In the gallery, I used to look with a great deal of interest at the paintings, especially those of a Russian painter named Nicholas Roerich and a Kerala painter named Raja Ravi Varma. Though he was a Russian, Roerich had decided to settle down in the foothills of the Himalayas. His son, Svetoslav Roerich, also an artist, came to India and he created quite a stir by marrying a glamorous screen star by the name of Devika Rani. Anyway, those infrequent visits to the gallery created an indelible impression in my mind and spawned a love for the visual arts. I can proudly say that I have been very lucky to visit many of the most famous galleries in the world. We have in our house many original paintings by Western Canadian artists.

It is rumored that my father baby-sat my mother. This was probably true because there was a difference of, I believe, seventeen years between them. My grandfather became a widower when my mother was five years old, and he was anxious to get on with his life and not bother about raising a girl. I am sure he wanted to get my mother off his hands as soon as was practicable. Perhaps my father did exactly that; I believe he waited until my mother finished her matriculation before suggesting marriage. In those days, many conservative families did not allow the girls to go to school, once they attained puberty. But I seriously doubt if my grandfather would have cared very much for social customs and strictures. I suspect they my parents had a civil marriage, because I don't remember anyone talking about any formal wedding ceremony.

My mother's father was a very senior official in the Ministry of Health. He was an imposing figure, a trained wrestler, and an expert in yoga, meditation, tantric rites, martial arts, and such. He was one of those "mind over matter" guys. Mother had related to me many stories of his control of the mind. I know for a fact that he stopped a rabid dog, which was rushing at him, by putting his hand out and staring at the dog. (Think Crocodile Dundee!) My father's brother was with him at that time and had witnessed the event.

My mother once told me of a surgery that was performed in her house. She was a young girl at that time. It appears that my grandfather developed a boil on his back. It became very large. It must have been very painful, but he ignored it and went about doing his business. At last, it reached a stage when it had to be surgically opened. But he refused to go to the hospital. He got the surgeon and nurse to come to his house.

He lay on the dining table and asked the surgeon to perform whatever he had to do. In those days, patients were given "ether" as an anesthetic. But he refused it, and he said he would give the signal when he was ready. He apparently lay down on his stomach, held on to the ends of the table, and after a few seconds, gave a grunt, signaling that the surgery could proceed. The surgery was performed, the wound bandaged, and he resumed his routine as if nothing had happened!

He was a bit of a rake also, as I understood later. He was married three times, though I don't recall meeting any of his wives. It appears that he went on this marrying spree after sending his daughter away. I also do not know what happened to them, because for a very long time, he lived by himself, as I recall. When he was in his late sixties, he married his fourth wife, a much younger woman. She was actually hired to be his housekeeper, but later on he married her, even though there was a difference of over thirty years between them. He had two children by her. The net result was that he gave away his considerable wealth to that woman, and my mother was cut off from his estate. He died when he was seventy-five.

Thus it was that neither of my parents got any inheritance of any kind.

My mother did not go beyond matriculation because, as I have said, her father probably got her married off. She was, however, among other things, very much interested in geography. One of her friends was a rich woman and, from her, she used to get back numbers of the *National Geographic*, which she would read from cover to cover. She would study atlases with a great deal of interest. Discovering a place, reading about it, and telling me all about it were a kind of ritual. She had such an enormous amount of trivia stored in her head—names of capitals, lengths of rivers, heights of mountains...

She was not very keen on gardening; and until I was grown up enough to do the chores, my father was the gardener-in-chief in the house. He had a neighbor's son come every day to water the plants. This was a big job, because the water had to be drawn from a very deep well.

By the 1950s, my father was getting tired of the effort involved in maintaining a good garden. I also could not do much because I was holding two jobs. In 1955, he leased the garden out to one of my neighbors who maintained the rose bushes but expanded the vegetable section. In 1958, my father sold the property and built a smaller house on a smaller lot about 100 meters from the old house. The new dwelling also would be called "Sukumara Park", though there was no "park" to speak of. Father had a few flowering perennials like oleander, hibiscus, jasmine and such. No roses!

My mother was a bit of a conservative and was very conscious of caste, one's place in the community. But she was no society woman by any means; we were not that wealthy. Later, I would realize that though we were not poor, we were not rich. I think I asked my father about this when I was growing up, and I recall being told that we were "middle class" people. Today, I think of the connotation of the term "middle class" and admit that it does not mean much, even if there is a standard with which to measure this status.

Poor, middle class, or whatever the status was, I knew that there were things that I wanted but could not afford. For instance, a tennis racket. I had a natural talent for playing tennis and ball badminton. (I am sure that not many of you know what ball badminton is! I am also sure that the game is not even played any more these days. Suffice it to say that you need a racket, a woolen ball, slightly smaller than a tennis ball, and a court, which is at least twice as long as the modern badminton court.) I believe I asked my parents why we did not do this or have that. There is nothing like an inquisitive child to make you realize just how complicated the topic of money is. Just as I asked my parents, my children had asked me at one time or another why we did not have two cars or a boat or why we did not go to Arizona or Florida every winter.[12]

I was quite young when my father's habit of smoking caught up with him. His constant coughing made everyone suspect that

12 I thought that I had my head around the nebulous term "middle class", until August 14, 2010, when I read the following, as reported by John Barber in the *Toronto Globe and Mail*. "British Prime Minister David Cameron set off a flurry of very British excitement this week when he referred to members of the 'sharp-elbowed middle classes like my wife and me' at a government-subsidized daycare centre. Noting his background and circumstances—son of a multimillionaire banker, educated at Eton and Oxford, married to the eldest daughter of a hereditary aristocrat—British pundits are perplexed."
Go figure!

he had perhaps contracted tuberculosis. I was twelve or so when a gloom descended on the Nair household; father was taken to a T.B.sanatorium, since his coughing reached alarming proportions. I remember that he went very early in the morning to the hospital some twenty miles away—which, in those days, was a great distance.

I also remember vividly that my mother was crying the whole day. The feeling was that he would never come back. But in the evening, my father sprinted down the long walkway from the gate shouting, "I don't have TB!"

He stopped smoking cold turkey, as the vernacular goes. But the bronchitis became a chronic condition.

My mother was a very beautiful woman. I suppose all mothers are! She had very long hair, so long that it reached almost to the mid calf region. She was very fond of sweet things. It was rumored that she would add sugar even in hot curries!! Well, one pays for such excesses; she developed diabetes before she reached fifty.

Even though I did not do her proud during my pre-Uganda days, later, when she found out that I was doing not too badly overseas, she would take every opportunity to trumpet my accomplishments. Unni (my pet name meaning "small, cute") did this, Unni did that and the other. He is in England, he is touring Europe, he is the Senior Master...

I was holidaying in India when I received the letter from the President of the College in Grande Prairie appointing me as Chairman of Continuing Education, and I saw firsthand how proud she was of me. She could not wait until she had told everybody about my "promotion". At that moment, her whole universe was centered on me. That year, when I was returning to Alberta, she took off her gold chain, something she wore always, and put it a round my neck. I still wear it.

She was in her late sixties when she died, due to complications arising from severe diabetes. I was not there when she passed away. She was in intensive care when she died and, apparently, she would ask often if I had been notified. Perhaps she had hoped that I might arrive to see her and that she might be able to see me once more for the last time.

My father was devastated. Though he lived up the ripe age of eighty-six, during that time he witnessed the death of several members of the family who were younger than him. This included his brother, all his cousins, their spouses, and a few of their children. He was a very religious man, and he deeply believed in the power of prayer and was willing to accept these losses as preordained. But when his life partner of almost six five decades passed away, not only did his resolve desert him, but a curious sense of anger at fate became quite evident, I was told, as if to ask why he had to be the one who had to bear all the sorrow. His meticulous routine was shattered, and people around him realized what *existing* was as opposed to *living*.

I could not go to India until about sixteen months after my mother died. What I saw shocked me! I hugged a frail man, reduced to skin and bones. It was very obvious that my father willed himself to live until he could see me once more.

Within three weeks of my arrival, he had a massive heart attack. Apparently, he had two mild ones immediately after my mother died. I rushed him to the hospital. I was due to leave within ten days. I spent the whole day before my departure with my father. Finally, it was time for me to go home and finish packing and get some rest before the flight early next morning.

I said, "You know, I am leaving tomorrow."

He just grunted. I asked him if that was all he had to say.

He said, "What is there to say? Did you not throw everything away and leave us?"

I realized, only then, that he had never actually relished my decision to leave him and the family. Needless to say, it hurt me to realize that my parents were not necessarily happy that I left them, to realize that, perhaps, I hurt them deeply. They let me go because I wanted to go.

I came home and wrote an obituary and gave it to my brother with instructions to publish it in all local newspapers when the time arrived. He was thunderstruck.

He said, "Are you crazy? He is still alive, for God's sake."

"Yes, he is. But he will not be...not for long," I said.

He died a few days after my departure.

When I think of my parents, I wonder what influence they had in my life. My father was a very disciplined man, with a lot of integrity. He was scrupulous. My mother was a very good manager, and this she showed during the war years.

If the fondness for reading is a genetic condition, I am sure I inherited it from my parents.

My parents never went outside the city in which they were born and where they spent all their life. They could not afford to take "holidays" or to "go on vacations". The farthest they went would have been to my uncle's farm some fifteen miles from where they lived.

One of the reasons for my going overseas was, among other things, to acquire financial strength to support my parents and help them to maintain a decent standard of living during their declining years. I knew I was not rich when I was growing up, and I did not want them to feel any strains brought on by monetary issues. So I wanted to support them as best as I could. This I did. If I had not, they would have had to eke out a living with my father's meager pension. My cousins and aunts and others had told me many times that *ammavan* and *ammavi* (uncle and auntie) were extremely lucky to have a son like me. I suppose they were right in a sense. But I also, perhaps, dashed their hopes. I did not become a high-ranking officer in the Auditor General's office. I suppose I could have, if I had stayed on. After all, I joined the department when I was in my twenties and was an officer in training. The regular promotion up the ladder would have made me at least the Deputy Auditor General. (In fact, one of the auditors who was recruited with me retired as the D.A.G.) So I wanted to make up for any disappointment they might have had, and I am sure I did it.

But in retrospect, I count my blessings. Had I not gone to Uganda, I would not have married Nalini, could not have accomplished all that I have over the last many decades.

Today, as I write this, I am reminded that I am the oldest living male in the family, and as my father did, I am having to watch many of the family—young and old—pass away. I have two female cousins who are older; but one of them is severely disabled, and the other one is very close to saying her good-byes. It is only a question of time.

My siblings

Nirmala Kumari (sister) and Radha Ramanan Nair (brother)

My sister was four or so years younger than me. I suspect that being older, I bullied her a bit—at least I was told this and was promptly punished for my bad behavior! She took music lessons with me, but I can't say that she was a gifted singer. She went to college and acquired a degree in history. But my parents did not allow her to seek a job, which perhaps was not a good thing. So she stayed home, helping mother with house hold chores, learning cooking, embroidery, and such. She was being groomed to be a good wife.

I left for Uganda three years after she finished her degree. She went through the normal routine of many Indian women—getting married, being a loving and loyal wife, raising children, and so on. A few years after her marriage, at my parents' request, she and her husband moved in with them. She passed away a couple of years ago. She was seventy-six. Her two children are well settled.

My brother was three years younger than my sister. He was the most active among us three. He could easily get into scrapes with neighboring children and had a short fuse! After completing college, he went to work for the State Transport Corporation.

He never got any formal music training, but he was a gifted singer—certainly better than me. He dabbled on the stage, as well. But he was an outstanding athlete, and he made his fame as a soccer international. He played in many state and national championships. He was picked to represent India in the Asian games, I believe, in 1956. I am afraid I have not had the thrill of watching him play, and I have knowledge of his achievements through paper cuttings that are preserved by his family.

After retiring from active soccer, he resigned from the Transport Corporation, as well, and was hired as Transport Officer in the newly formed Indian Space Research Organization.

My brother also passed away four years ago. He was seventy.

His two children are well settled.

My siblings were very loyal to me, loved me immensely, were proud of what I had accomplished, and were grateful for all the help I had given to the family, in general, and them in particular. I want to say with pride and warmth that their children also love and respect me very much, and I am grateful.

My In-laws

<u>Mr. Keshavlal Oza and Mrs. Savitri Oza</u>

We called them Motabhai and Ba. They are both deceased. I must say that I am proud to have known them. During the pre-independence days, my father-in-law was a Dewan (Prime Minister) of one of the states in Saurashtra, now part of the state of Gujarat. (India had over five hundred states, some deemed first class. Mr. Oza was the Dewan of one of the first-class states.) After independence, the states were dissolved, the kings paid a pension, and the map of the country redrawn on linguistic lines. But Mr. Oza stayed on to manage the affairs of the king. He was a lawyer by training.

I had never met a more distinguished-looking man. He was smallish but exuded a great deal of gravitas. He had a serious mien; he was not given to small talk and was the patriarch of the family. Ba was many years younger than Motabhai, just as my mother was. She was a very educated person, but she devoted her time in raising her children and being a good companion for her husband. Graceful and gracious, she was one of the most loving people I have ever met.

What was surprising (for me) was that both of them embraced me into the family without any question, even though I was from a different race and different caste. They loved me very dearly. I know this for a fact, because others in the family never tire of telling me this. I must say that I was very nervous when I first I met them. We did not speak the same language (not that it affected communication, because most in the family spoke English), our food habits were different, and our cultural beliefs were different. And yet, I was accepted without any question whatever; and I am proud to say that I did not cause any grief or give them any anxious moments.

Motabhai was a very religious person like my father. He spent the last several years of his life administering an Ashram[13], recruiting young men to be trained as priests. He also started an educational foundation.

My wife
Nalini Nayar

My wife and I came our several ways and met in Kampala. Her ambition was to work in Uganda for a few years, make some money, and go back to her home state of Gujarat and start a school for girls. But the best-laid plans went awry because I interfered! She came from a large family—four brothers and two sisters. With all the boys around her, I suspect she might have had to fight for her turf, because one of the most endearing qualities of my wife is that, though she has a heart of gold, she has a steely determination. She

---

13 Traditionally an ashram is a religious hermitage. Additionally, today, the term often denotes a locus of Indian cultural activity, such as yoga, music study, or religious instruction.

is feisty. These qualities were obvious to me when I first came to know her, and it was a charming experience courting her.

She came from a very distinguished and highly educated family. One of her uncles was a shipping magnate and another chief prosecutor of the erstwhile state of Bombay. One of her brothers was a banker, another a cardiologist. A third one was a highly-placed civil servant, and yet another was a professor of economics at a university in Gujarat. One of the sisters was a teacher and another took pleasure in just being a housewife and mother. At one time, there were fifteen doctors in the clan—counting cousins, uncles, and aunts.

Nalini was a reputed teacher in Uganda, and when we moved to Alberta, she taught in the same school where I was the Principal. She retired as an instructor at the Grande Prairie Regional College. She was a specialist in Reading. She was easily one of the most popular instructors in the college.

She supported me in all my extra-curricular activities. She shared my passion for traveling. She got involved in theatre as a producer for several shows of the GPLT; she did the publicity for all my shows.

But deep down, she is an artist. She probably would have made an excellent interior designer. Her touch is always obvious in the house; and she is forever changing things around, decorating our house with all the several dozen artifacts we have collected from around the world. She still collects *objets d'art* whenever possible. She is also an avid reader.

The way my own career shaped up, I had to leave home very often, and thus I dumped on her the daily chores, like driving the kids to hockey, to music lessons, and such. This she did without grudge, even though minor health issues might have dampened the zeal. To the kids, she was a giving and caring mother and, to me, she was a counsellor, friend, and mate. Recently, she has taken on the role of the manager of our investments. For this, she taught herself the intricacies of markets and learned to deal with their erratic behavior.

But it is in her role as a mother that she excelled. I suppose all mothers would take credit for this; but my wife truly practiced tough love. I believe my children do feel very lucky to have her as their mother, as I do to have her as my wife. Her influence on me has been wholly beneficial.

My children

Nikku Nayar (son) and Radha Nayar (daughter)

The observations that follow regarding the attitude of parents strictly reflect my Indian bias and my own upbringing, meaning it may or may not be true of others.

I believe that all parents, wherever they come from, want their children to pursue careers, which give them an ability to live a better life than that they themselves had. It is also true that many parents would like their children to pursue the same career they did. My father certainly did. He was sure that I could reach the highest cadre of the civil service. He perhaps wanted to enjoy the perch vicariously.

Indian parents also, generally, have a habit of defining or influencing the career of their children. Careers in medical, engineering and, these days, IT professions are usually at the top of the list. But it is also true that no Indian parent would seriously demand that the children turn out to be teachers, unless the teaching position is in a college or university. Here is a strange paradox. Teaching is a profession that produces professionals in all fields of human endeavor and yet, teaching school is *infra dig!*

This is because the financial returns are not great, and in a society that is obsessed with class and caste and such aberrations, teachers do not enjoy the prestige that doctors, engineers and such enjoy. In Canada, the legal profession is very lucrative, but when I was growing up, not many Indian lawyers that I knew of made a decent living. There were too many lawyers, I guess; and only the smartest and gifted made it big.

Nalini and I had decided very early that the kids should be allowed to choose their own paths as far as a career is concerned, and they did.

Nikku grew up like any other Canadian boy, doing the things that other kids did, except that he was much better than others in whatever he participated in. So, sometimes, we thought he would be a great mathematician! Sometimes, we thought that he would be a professional golfer or basketball player. But he chose to be a musician. I was only painfully aware of the cut-throat competition in the performing arts business, how there are thousands of musicians who want to be successful like many hundred recording artists who are widely and wildly famous. As the cliché goes, it is all about being at the right place and being spotted by the right person. He stuck with it, went through a baptism of fire like any artist and, we are happy and proud to say that he has been highly successful. He is a busy jobbing musician in Toronto. He is also a regular touring member of Kiran Ahluwalia's band. (Kiran is a Juno award-winning singer based in New York.) He frequently travels to Europe to accompany Kiran. He also maintains an active teaching practice in Toronto.

Radha showed equal promise, excelled in academic work and anything else she set her heart on. I suspect she did not like blood, and so she did not what to be a doctor! She was a natural athlete and I recall that she almost singlehandedly won the trophy for her school in the inter-school track and field competition for elementary schools. She was given the honor of doing the victory lap. She has great facility in the use of English and, at one point, I thought that she might major in English. She exhibited her academic strength when she scored a GPA of 3.95 for her graduate degree in Social Work. She is an accomplished musician, has a great singing voice and, at one time, played piano, oboe, and the violin. But she chose to become a social worker, because she is a very compassionate person. She earns her living as a private consultant in the non-profit sector. She is highly successful in her career. She has kept her musical interest alive by singing in a local choir in Toronto.

While growing up, both kids competed in the provincial festival in such categories as music, story telling, musical theatre, and monologues. They invariably placed first every year they competed. Both kids had the opportunity to appear on the stage in suitable roles.

Needless to say, both of them have done us proud. It is not every parent who could say this with conviction. Whatever their accomplishments, Nalini and I take comfort in the fact that both of them would be available to take care of us in our days of infirmity.

We have been denied the pleasure of being grandparents—yet—but that is a small issue.

Mr. Kesavan Nair

Mr. Nair was my friend, counsellor, and mentor. He was an elder brother I never had. He was known as Victory Kesavan Nair, because he was the owner and manager of The Victory Tutorial College in the city. It was in this college that I got the opportunity to teach English. Mr. Nair was an extraordinary man, but he was an ordinary clerk in the Kerala government service. I am sure that no one in my family living today has even heard of him. But when he was alive, he was one of the most influential men in the city. He intimately knew many people from the upper echelons to the lowest of the low! I am not sure how he acquired such tremendous influence; he certainly was not a very wealthy person. I believe that he used people to help other people. So one was always "obligated" to him. For example, the Head of a given department in the government would have a son who was weak in, say, English, and he would ask me if I would help the kid. In return, the passage of my passport application and income tax clearance certificate and such annoying thickets would be cleared easily. This is just one example, although it might appear trite. He had an army of helpers to cater to an equally large number of "helpees". If you wanted anything, you went to Mr. Nair.

The Victory Tutorial College was essentially meant for preparing students for matriculation and college degree examinations. The students, some of them regular college goers, came for private tuition and extra help. We had a large number of students. I recall that one of my English classes was close to eighty students.

Unfortunately, he suffered from chronic tuberculosis, and only heavy doses of medication kept him alive. Because of his immense influence in the medical community, he had a large number of medical practitioners who used their collective skills to "take care" of him. But in the fifties, there were not many sophisticated or efficacious medicines available for TB.

In 1959, I was on home leave, and he came to say good-bye on the day I was due to depart for Uganda. He embraced me, for the first time ever, and said that it was unlikely that we would meet again. I did not say anything. I could not, because I was too over-come with emotions. He died two years later.

In addition to mentoring me, he also let me take responsibili-ties related to the administration of the college. This was mostly because of his failing health. Thus, I developed the ability to man-age administrative affairs and deal with personnel. I also devel-oped my skills in communication and learned the art of morale building.

Noam Chomsky

Perhaps you know Chomsky as a political activist. Maybe some of you remember him as the foremost linguist of his time.

I consider myself privileged to have taken a course from him. It was during this time that I learned that English has, indeed, a grammar that makes sense! I don't want to go into the details of the inherent flaws in English grammar, except to say that I, perhaps like you, have been frustrated with the "rules" of the English lan-guage. For me, it was all the more confusing because Malayalam, my mother tongue, has rules that make sense! Obviously, because of its roots in Sanskrit, which has the most comprehensive and sensible grammar ever written, explained by a man called Panini.[14] Drawing inspiration and knowledge from Panini's work, Chomsky

---

14   Panini. Ancient Sanskrit grammarian (circa fourth century B.C.E.) wrote the earliest known work on descriptive linguistics and generative linguistics. His sophisticated and logical rules and technique have been widely influential in modern linguistics.

revolutionized rules of English grammar. He also created the term psycholinguistics.

Richard Schechner

Dr. Schechner was my teacher when I was a student at New York University doing post-graduate work in theatre. He conceptualized a somewhat eclectic area of theatre studies called "Performance Theory" and is the leading expert in the field.

But what impressed me about him was his vast knowledge of Indian mythology and expertise in Indian dance/theatre forms. He was an expert on Ramleela, an annual Indian pageant which celebrates the story of Rama, the hero of Ramayana, one of the epic poems in Indian literature. Ramleela is very much like the Passion play performed in Oberammergau, except that it happens every year. The whole village participates in the pageant, and it annually attracts thousands of visitors, worshippers, thespians, and experts.

People who become scholars in fields that are indigenous to a different culture always impress me. The first Malayalam-English dictionary was written, not by a Keralite, but a German, Gunter Stephenson. The first Sanskrit-English dictionary was written, not by an Indian, but by Monier Williams, who was the professor of Sanskrit at Oxford! Both these "events" happened in the mid-nineteen hundreds.

Dr. Schechner's knowledge of Indian mythology and Natyasastra (an ancient Indian treatise on the performing arts, encompassing theatre, dance, and music, probably written around 200 BCE) is profound. I admire him for his scholarship and deep personal qualities. I am proud to consider him a friend.

I particularly cherish a letter in which he said, among other things, "Your cultural status is so beautifully complex…"

Dr. Sophie Freud

Dr. Freud is the granddaughter of the great Sigmund himself. I had the privilege of meeting her when I was in High Level. She was visiting Grouard, in Alberta, to hold a workshop for the women on the Indian reservation. At that time, she was a professor at the prestigious Simmons College in Boston, Massachusetts.

I came to know of her visit from the chief of the Cree Indians in the region, and he wondered if Fairview College would sponsor a visit to High Level, considering that I had many native Indian students in the various centers. I got her on the phone and she was surprisingly amenable to the idea of visiting the town.

She spent two days with us, visiting three of the fifteen centers in my jurisdiction. She had such a charming empathy when she talked to the native women.

What I remember most during the visit was that, as soon as we shook hands, she said, "I am a Freud but not a Freudian. Don't talk about my grandfather!" I was so disappointed. I was hoping that I could get some firsthand insight about the man!

She stayed with me and we had conversations going very late into the night. She liked hot curries too!

Such an incisive, probing mind!

Peter Brook

Peter Brook is a theatre and film director and innovator from England. This Oxonian is one of the most respected directors of Shakespeare. He is also known for producing a play based on the epic *Mahabharata*, which is the longest poem written in any language. It is ten times as long as the *Iliad* and the *Odyssey* combined. He reduced this massive tome into a play running for nine hours.

In 1980, he came to New York with his play *A Conference of the Birds.*

Dr. Schechner invited Brook to give us a workshop, mostly on his play and his seminal work *The Empty Space.* From the perspective of a theatre buff, the experience was extraordinary.

He put me to shame by asking me to explain one of the most important rituals—Ashwamedha—described in *Mahabharata.* I suppose he asked me because I am an Indian. I believe I gave a very shoddy description, mostly because I did not know the details! Brook has a pair of piercing blue eyes. He uses them to cow you or give a mischievous smile. I believe I got a smile.

Victor Turner

Victor Turner was a British anthropologist, best known for his work on symbols, rituals, and rites of passage. Dr. Richard Schechner drew from Turner's theories on social drama and "liminality". (A liminal phase is between rites of passage.) He happened to be in New York in 1980, and it was only natural that he would be invited to talk to Schechner's students. Richard told Dr. Turner about my interest in masks and rituals, and so he graciously agreed to spend some time with me...all of five minutes! He said something to the effect that India is a land of intriguing rituals, but regrettably, he had not been able to find time to study them, because he had been concentrating on African rituals. He asked me what I was working on and wished me good luck. He would die within three years, in 1983. He was sixty-five.

Before I am accused of name dropping, let me conclude by quoting a couple of lines from the British poet Stephen Spender. The title of the poem is *"I Think Continually Of Those Who Were Truly Great"*.

"I think continually of those who were truly great...Born of the sun they travelled a short while towards the sun, and signed the vivid air with their honour."

For me, the time spent with these great people has been extra ordinarily stimulating; the experience has been unforgettable. I consider myself extremely lucky.

CHAPTER SEVEN

AN ADDENDUM, SORT OF

On revisiting the narrative written so far, I have noticed that I had not paid attention to three elements in the "amorphous mass" that I had referred to earlier on.

The first has to do with my acting stint in India and here in Canada. As I had mentioned, my stage experience in India had been limited to playing female roles. I had had many interesting experiences; but one, I believe, takes the cake. A distant relative of my father had some kind of a special function in his house. It was to be held in the evening. But that particular evening, I had a performance, and so I was told that he would send his car and I should not bother to change from my costume—an easy act that could be performed in the car! So, after the show, I rushed backstage, picked up my bag, and went to the alley behind the theatre where the car was parked. In the front, it would have been very crowded. When I was walking toward the car, I saw a man approach me. It was a darkish lane, and when he was close, I was sure he was going to attack me. I told him that I was not really a woman. He muttered something to the effect, "We shall soon see."

Then he gripped my blouse and pulled it down, and out popped two tennis balls!

I had never seen a man retract and run so fast!

Though it was as a director that I made a name for myself, I have been fortunate to perform a few memorable roles on the Grande Prairie stage. Of course, many directors were loath to cast me in a role that requires blue eyed, blonde men, even though they were aware that I had more than average acting skills. I am not sure I blame them because, being a purist, I always respected the essence and integrity of the script, and as such, I would not have cast someone who did not "look" the role. As I had mentioned earlier, I don't think it is "right" for a white man to play Othello, though many of the top ranking actors have attempted to play the role. So I had to audition for the roles that were "right" for me. The first such role—that of a Greek, Victor Velasco—came in the Neil Simon's comedy *Barefoot in the Park*. This was, I believe, in 1977. The play was mounted again in 2004, and I reprised the role. By then, I had grayed so much, the director had my hair and beard dyed. The day after closing, I was due to fly to Russia, and I thought that I had better take photos of my face—before and after dyeing. As it happened, it was a wise move because, sure enough, the immigration authorities at Moscow airport had eyebrows raised when they looked at me and the picture in the passport. I showed them the pictures and tried to explain what had happened.

I got another chance to perform in a very good play called *The Gin Game,* in which I got to act as a resident in an old folks' home. It is a powerful play.

But the most satisfying role was in a play called *Death and the Maiden.* I was cast in the role of a sadistic doctor in Chile, during the time of Pinochet. As it happens he, by chance, arrives at the house of one of the victims of his torture and is gagged and bound. The victim, the housewife, is determined to shoot him. There is one scene where she pokes the doctor very hard on his back with the gun. This scene was rehearsed literally a hundred times so that the poke lands beside the backbone. One night, the lady playing the role seemingly lost control and hit me right on the vertebra. It hurt, of course; the audience chalked up the resultant pain on my face to a brilliant piece of acting! The damage still acts up when the weather is cold!

There have been many shows in which I played bit parts for the fun of it. In retrospect, I believe I enjoyed acting more than directing.

The second activity that had consumed a large part of my life was playing tennis and watching professionals in action. I believe I had mentioned that I was better than an average player, and I am positive that, during the early days, if I had been able to afford a good racket and basic coaching, I might have gone far. I played active tennis above the club level until I moved to Boyle. Though I participated in many tournaments, I have no trophy to testify to my expertise in this sublime game. But that does not matter; I enjoyed my time on the unique, well-defined rectangle.

Watching good tennis is equally as satisfying as playing, and I consider myself extremely lucky to have seen three of the four grand slams—Wimbledon three times, the US Open two times, and the French Open once. Though we had been to Melbourne, we could not align our trip with the grand slam there, and so that event has remained elusive.

I cannot think of any major player that I have not seen in action, starting with the greats like Ramanathan Krishnan, Pancho Gonzales, and Rod Laver. I am going out on a limb to say that Roger Federer is the best player of all time, and no one is going to match his expertise...ever! I realize that this blatant statement is bound to raise arguments from my daughter, who adores Raphael Nadal!

Finally, I have to mention an activity that I had pursued for over ten years without break—except when I was indisposed or was on foreign assignments. This was writing a weekly column for the Friday supplement of the local newspaper in Grande Prairie, *The*

Daily Herald Tribune. Under the not too original title **"Subtext"**, I let my mind wander on a wide variety of themes from garage sales, to Camus, to funeral rites in Bali, to my meeting with Dr. Dubov. When I argued that mutton is goat meat, the Publisher had angry letters from the Grande Prairie Sheep Growers' Association. I let my flights of fancy soar about each of the cardinal numbers from zero to nine. (Ten is still waiting to be explored.) I wrote my last article in August 2009.

Sometimes, I had wondered if I should not have been a writer, perhaps chosen journalism as a career, but I probably would not have received any encouragement from my father!

One of the articles appears as Appendix Two.

CHAPTER EIGHT

THROUGH COLORED GLASSES

So far, you have been reading what I had to say about myself. So it just might be appropriate if I documented what others think of me.

Over the years, after an exhausting production, I would announce that it would be my swan song. But invariably, especially after an overseas assignment, the itch would come again, and I would announce yet another show. Thus, my "swan song" became a topic of jokes among friends!

After one such self-imposed closure, the local newspaper sent Christina Grant to interview me and write a story on my "retirement". I believe this was in May 1998. For the material for her article, she picked a few local thespians and asked all of them a set of three questions. The buildup to the questionnaire and the answers are on the next page.

AND THE DIRECTOR CALLED CUT!

Sukumar Nayar retires
(and other fables from live theatre in Grande Prairie)

By *Christina Grant.*

(What follows are excerpts from the article.)

Sukumar Nayar, one of the steadiest and brightest lights on the Grande Prairie stage for twenty-eight years, has announced his "official" retirement, as he closes in on age seventy. But nobody is buying it.

"I'm tired," the slight, bespectacled man sighs over coffee at the Pepper Pot. "During the production of *The Comedy of Errors*, I discovered that the process and the experience are not challenging anymore. Although the play was immensely rewarding, it wasn't fun."

And without that, he says, there's no point. He treated the experience as a subliminal hint that he should either stop or give it a rest. I prefer to stop. From now on, I would only get involved if something truly challenging comes along...

Any regrets; anything he really wanted to tackle and never did?

"No," he says remarkably quickly. "If I wanted to do something, I did it."

Indeed, he's pretty much famous locally for pushing the envelope...

"I learned something new from each show I did," Sukumar says. "It's made me very humble."

One of the things he seems most proud of is the casting of beginners. "Almost every show I had done, I put in a rookie actor. It was important. If I didn't give them a chance, who would..."

WHAT PEOPLE SAY ABOUT SUKUMAR NAYAR:
THE MAN

Wayne Ayling: Lawyer, Ex Mayor of Grande Prairie

Sukumar Nayar is a human dynamo, filled with effervescence and determination.

Dr. Jack Wynters: Medico and Professional actor

I don't know a nicer, gentler person. He exudes gentleness and generosity; there is always a wonderful note of serenity around him, and he takes that into whatever sphere he engages in. That's a quality not many have. I don't think I've ever heard him say an evil word about anyone.

Kathy Harper: Actor, Director

He may be small in stature, but he has an absolutely huge mind. He has an amazing memory, and out of that memory spills the most beautiful words. I just love listening to him talk. Sukumar has the most powerful love of language; he always seems to have the right words for every occasion.

Jenny Tetreau: Actor, Director

A reliable, true friend.

Jim Nelson: Actor, raconteur, playwright, director, musician

He's industrious, meticulous, restless, easily bored and a world citizen.

Tom Hawkesworth: Chief Crown Prosecutor, actor, director

Sukumar and Nalini are two of the most charming people I've ever met, always very encouraging and hospitable.

Dr. Henry Anderson: Ex President, Grande Prairie Regional College, scholar, visionary

We are of almost identical age, and we have an affinity for how we look at the world, although we stand at different points. Sukumar is a great humanist. He's a very insightful man, and that shows up in the way he handles people—observing and respecting them—the essential elements of a good teacher. He was an extraordinarily important member of the college community—a kind of council of colleagues. Sukumar is a good man. Most of us would be happy to have that on our epitaph.

THE ACTOR/ DIRECTOR

Wayne Ayling

He's sensitive to important issues facing human beings as a society and is always prepared to focus an audience's attention on those strong issues.

Dr. Jack Wynters

Sukumar is a great dreamer. He'll come up with a scheme and make it happen. Some are detail people; they do the running around and organizing. He dreams it up in the first place and has the communication skills to get other people enthusiastic. As a director, he is exceptionally generous. He lets the actors find the approach to the role; he does not impose his ideas. He may suggest things, but he never puts his foot down, unless the production is in jeopardy.

Kathy Harper

As a director he knows exactly what he wants and has a beautiful way of making people think that they discovered it themselves. It's truly a gift. He has never been intrusive or authoritarian, and because of that, people are encouraged to keep on with it. He has always really helped actors with self-discovery, and when you discover things yourself, it remains with you longer. That is his legacy.

Jenny Tetreau

As a director, he never tells you when you are doing right. If you don't know that about him, it can be kind of alarming. But for sure, you will know if you are doing something that is not quite what he had in mind. He will make a lot of suggestions.

He is wonderful to be on stage with as an actor. He is very giving. Sukumar brings out the best in fellow actors, because he knows when the focus should be on them. He makes you look good.

Jim Nelson

As a person of theatre, he's easily one of the most well-read people I've ever met. As a director, he tends to typecast physically and let the chips fall as they may. So over the years, anybody could try any role, but he was fiercely loyal to the production.

Tom Hawkesworth

He's very easy to work with, both as an actor and as a director. He manages to get it all going without making any kind of ordeal. Besides the habit of making his name bigger than the playwright's in the playbill, he does not have a big ego! He directs in a very humble way. He wants to put on a good show and have fun, so there is no wasted effort.

Dr. Henry Anderson

As a director, he allowed people to express and interpret their characters; he did not tell them who their characters were. Also, he provided an opportunity for people to see productions you would not normally expect to appear in Grande Prairie. People had to reach above themselves in his productions.

Sukumar helped people to dare. And he felt that if you dare, you should dare greatly. He should be respected now that he has said that he is retiring from theatre. While theatre is much of him, it's not all of him.

SPECIAL MOMENT

Wayne Ayling

Despite his long experience, he is very much a worrywart. But worrying is a symptom of his enthusiasm. He will agonize over the tiniest detail.

Dr. Jack Wynters

There have been so many with Sukumar. He is such a special person. I have enjoyed a long, satisfying, gentle relationship with him that has been very rewarding.

Kathy Harper

In 1971, when he first came to Grande Prairie, he knocked on my door, introduced himself, and said that he was doing *Hedda Gabler* by Henrik Ibsen and said that he would like me to play the lead role. I had never acted before and Hedda is considered one of the great roles for women. Eight hundred and ten lines later, I was into theatre. It is because of him I'm still doing it, and there are many more stories like this out there.

Jenny Tetreau

> He scared the hell out of me in *The Gin Game*, when he pounded the card table with his cane so hard, it collapsed. One night, he put a hole right through it. I didn't have to act; I was really frightened.

Jim Nelson

> A whole gang of us was on the road taking a show to Medicine Hat, Alberta. We stopped for lunch, and Sukumar ordered soup with extra crackers and more extra crackers. We all got involved in one of our erudite, engrossing conversations, when I gradually became aware of him sitting in his chair with his head cocked back, staring directly at the ceiling. With great concentration, he was placing one cracker after another on his forehead, balancing them there, all the while carrying on with the conversation. Finally, when the stack was high enough, in one deft action and with one hand, he smashed all the crackers, leaned forward and they all fell into his soup. He must have been practicing this for years. At that moment, I realized that there was more to this man than met the eye.

Dr. Henry Anderson

> I stayed with him while he was on sabbatical from the college, studying at New York University. To hear him so caught up in what he was doing was a special time. There he was in his pure element. Sukumar in theatre was the real Sukumar. Not all of us find the milieu in which we are our best selves.

CHAPTER NINE

POSTSCRIPT

While reminiscing about my busy life, I have often wondered who or what exactly I am. Am I just a teacher? Or am I polyglot who would have learned another six or seven languages if I had the opportunity? And am I so consumed with wanderlust that I would have traveled to yet another forty-one countries? Am I a born administrator and, by extension, a leader? Am I, deep down, a thespian who would embrace theatre as a religion? Or am I just another ordinary Canadian of Indian origin?

I want to think of myself as just a teacher. After I joined the Grande Prairie Regional College, I made it a habit of getting the students to evaluate my performance in every course that I had taught over the years. Until I got my tenure, it was mandatory. But I continued to get the reactions from students, even when their evaluation did not serve any official purpose or satisfy some policy dictate. It was a self-education mechanism. I wanted to know what I needed to concentrate on, where to revisit pedagogical matters, where to strengthen my grasp of the subject.

I must say that I got uniformly encouraging feedback from students. Many students occasionally recall their brief association with me. A few, like professional actor Alex Zahara, never tire of praising me and acknowledging that I touched many very deeply. I want to end this with a couple of reactions. One is a story, and another is part of a letter.

Many years ago, one of our friends in Grande Prairie, Dr. Sam Dube went to Winnipeg for a Medical conference of some kind. During dinner, he and his wife Pushpa were seated next to an Indian couple, Dr. and Mrs. Pravin Mehta. During the course of the meal, when Dr. Mehta learned that Sam was from Grande Prairie, he asked if he knew of a man called Sukumar Nayar. Later, Pravin would tell Sam, "Mr. Nayar was my teacher in Uganda, and I would never have gone to medical school but for him. He taught us English and Health Science. The way he explained how the body works, I got fascinated with human biology, and I decided that I would become a doctor." Pravin went to London to get his medical degree. I did meet him many years ago in Winnipeg where he had already established himself as a reputable doctor. His wife Kalpana also was my student.

The part of the letter that follows is from Cliff Mitchell. He was, among other things, expressing his regrets for not being able to attend a farewell given by friends of the theatre in Grande Prairie.

"You need to know how much you have affected me and Joyce. You gave me hope when I doubted. Back in college in the fall of 1977 in your drama class, I rejoined the human race. I developed a feeling of self-worth that changed my life. I was at a huge threshold in my life, and you helped me to take the necessary steps that not only affected my career but my entire life. I had begun to feel that I didn't matter so much. Your class and your faith in me to take on a huge role in An Enemy of the People, *and the acceptance by the school and the audience gave me the impetus to persevere and go ahead with my life in a positive direction..."*

APPENDICES

APPENDIX ONE

(The following is a report that appeared in the local newspaper, The Daily Herald Tribune, *Grande Prairie, August 2009)*
COLUMN: Best. of luck in the Big Smoke to Sukumar and Nalini Nayar

Fred Rinne – Our Community

There are certain people we meet in this crazy life who, it seems to me, do their best work when you start off by telling them it can't be done.

Sukumar Nayar is one of those people.

For thirty-nine years he has shared his thespian excellence with Grande Prairie and area theatre-goers, creating an eclectic cornucopia of staging that are too complicated and numerous to qualify here.

And that's a microcosm of the man.

Born and raised in India, the son of a modest civil servant who had a love of live theatre, Suk was introduced (laughingly, as he describes it) to the art at a very young age, when he was included in a production that, for him, involved just one line – which he flubbed. And so the legend began.

His career took him to Uganda and then to Canada to Boyle, Alberta, initially. Immediately, he sought to liven the local stage scene and has been doing so ever since.

Sukumar and his wonderful wife Nalini moved to our city in 1971. Sukumar was hired as an English teacher at the Grande Prairie Regional College (whose first home was the old Central Park school downtown), which then also had space at a site roughly in the area of the parking lot of St. Joseph church.

Immediately, Nayar put his indelible imprint on the city's theatre scene. He staged *The Ecstasy of Rita Joe*—an ultra-important Canadian play dealing with the plight of our aboriginal people, which includes a scene with the sexual assault of a native girl. Unthinkable. Preposterous. Can't be done. Did.

And over the course of the next four decades, the best way to motivate Sukumar was tell him he couldn't do it.

Bring on the College Players, GPLT, Highway 40 Productions, Broadway Live Broadway, among others, and the legacy lives on undeniably.

Last Sunday, a gathering of nearly seventy at Second Street Theatre applauded the efforts of both Sukumar and Nalini, the beautiful and strong, silent type (aka the brains of the operation), as a walk down memory script was tactfully handled by Wade Fleming.

Fans and friends from near and far attended, many traveling great distances to be there, including Marie Nychka from Edmonton and Pearl and Gerald Baldwin from Nanaimo, B.C.

At the end of the GP day, one hundred, fifty stage productions share the Nayar name. Do the math and that means almost three a year, every year, on average. And anyone involved in a production knows the run of a play is the tip of the iceberg. Seventy percent of it is under the water. Amazing stuff.

I loved many of Sukumar's projects in the years I have been here, but I am partial to *Jesus Christ Superstar*, which he did twice. It was fitting to see *JC* of stage and local mural meister Tim Heimdal at the event, resurrected as the lead in almost bookend productions of the Nayar stage experience.

There were so many wonderful people at the event, we don't have space to mention them all, but we should ask GPLT manager Rick Hryciuk, Wade Fleming, Margaret Wright, Lorraine Cook, Monica Benning, Kelvin and Vikki Potter, Jenny Tetreau, and Tracy Sauchenko to take a curtain call of thanks for the event.

Sukumar wrote **Subtext** for various incarnations of our paper for the better part of a decade, and he always challenged me as an editor, pushing the envelope, trying to convince me tennis was art and George W. Bush was wicked. We agreed to disagree on the basis of crafting principles. I hope the mutual respect will always be there for a man entrusted by the United Nations to head up world missions.

Sukumar and Nalini leave near month's end for Toronto to be nearer to their family. As Nalini told us, she grew up in a massive city in India and finally got used to life here and now back again.

C'est la vie, eh?

As I pen this column, I am listening to an audio track of *JC Superstar*, as mentioned, the shining star of Sukumar's local resumé in my opinion.

And on that note, my friends, I will miss you.

It was thirteen years ago when we met, but, "After all, it seems like thirty, seems like ninety."

In reality, it seems like yesterday.

Farewell.

APPENDIX TWO

(One of the articles that I wrote for the weekly supplement of the local newspaper)
SUBTEXT for December 4, 2008

Sukumar Nayar

The latest craze in Kenya is to give newborn babies (and the not so newborn, as well) the name "Barack Obama". The Kenyans consider Obama their own, though he was not born in Kenya and though his ties with that country have been limited. His father was a Kenyan who, as it happens, abandoned the president-elect before he was born. Well, I guess there is a justifiable pride and reason for a Kenyan naming a child Barack Obama. Kenya has declared the 4th of November a National holiday.

Names have always fascinated me or rather why people give their children the names they give. Sarah McLachlan, the great Canadian singer named her daughter "India". Can you imagine going through life with the name "Turkey"?

Anyway, what inspired me to write this article was something not exactly spectacular. Sometimes on CNN, I had noticed that the news anchor in the evening was a handsome black American by the name of Don Lemon. I was mildly curious at the last name. Then a few weeks later, a lady appeared on PBS and her name is Mary Money. These names are not meaningless; but how does one acquire them? That intrigued me.

We all know that the last name or surname or family name is a fixed name shared with the members of a family and is passed on from generation to generation. We also know that women—most women—when they get married, surrender the family name they were born with—a brutal affliction I might add. Who would want to go through life with the name Mrs. Nayar?!

It appears that the use of surnames is relatively new in history and was adopted in order to legally distinguish two individuals with the same first name. When I say "new", I mean at least the 14th century, because we know that Geoffrey Chaucer (circa 1345) was the son of John Chaucer.

The Chinese were among the first culture to adopt the use of hereditary surnames about 5000 years ago.

During my student days, I had been introduced to the various surnames through literature and history. So Dickens, Wordsworth, Keats, Heathcliff, Carton, and such names were taken for granted. I must admit I did not bother to find out what they really "meant", if anything. I had an idea that Dickens had something to do with Dick, perhaps; but I had no idea what Keats meant. I still don't. But what triggered my thinking was my first visit to the Central railway station in the capital city of the state in which I was born. I must have been fourteen or so and I had never been to a railway station before; I had no need to.

One of the lasting legacies of the British in India was the introduction of the railway system, and every major station had on the platform two institutions. One was Higginbottoms, a small store that sold newspapers, magazines, cookies, chocolates, smokes, and such. The other was a Western-style restaurant that served Western food and where the natives learned the use of knives and forks. They were both on the platform, and so admission was restricted to passengers or those who came to receive/see off people.

The name Higginbottoms intrigued me. Somebody's bottom?! Could that be a name? Indeed it was. The owner, Richard, had a chain of such kiosks all over the country. In fact, major cities had a Higginbottoms bookstore as well. They still do, though I believe they have changed the name to Higginbothams.

It was not until I got acquainted with the humorist P. G. Wodehouse in my late teens that I learned about really "funny" or "strange" surnames. I am not sure whether the immortal names he introduced his fans to were real. I suspect not. It had to be the creation of a comic genius. I cannot imagine someone going around with names such as Augustus Fink-Nottle, P. P. Purkiss, Honora Glossop, Esmond Haddock, Bertram Wooster and, of course, Jeeves. (The first name of Jeeves is "Reginald".)

Surname spelling has evolved over centuries and, until the 20th century, the spelling of a surname was not fixed. Before then, it was not unusual to see the same person's surname spelled in different ways from record to record (Cook vs. Cooke or Pool vs. Poole). In the 1800s and before, when many people were illiterate, names were written by clerks, officials, and priests, as they heard the name pronounced. This led to different spellings for the same name. My own name should have been "Nair", but somehow it got to be "Nayar". Spelling continued to evolve until the last century. This perhaps explains why the Obama's National Finance Director's name is spelled Juliana Smoot. I suspect it was "smooth" a few centuries ago.

I have also noticed that many Jewish last names refer to metals and precious stones: gold (Golda), silver, ruby, diamond.

Maybe it was Wodehouse who prompted me to go to the computer and look for "strange" surnames. The list I got is astonishingly long. Here is a sampling:

Amblyne, Diddams, Figgatt, Ingledent, Istead, Koputh, Levise, Pheasey, Pottoe, Tearce, Titmouse, Uniacke, Vertigans, and Yapp.

These are names listed by the Gloucester family History Society, if you are interested.

Well, what is there in a name, right? And some would say "Nayar" is a strange name. At least it is the only one here in Grande Prairie.

APPENDIX THREE

AWARDS

I have already mentioned some of the awards I have received, and they appear in some context or the other. I am listing them again for easy reference.

Distinguished Services Medal from the British Government, awarded in 1962 on the eve of Uganda's independence.

Gold Medal from the Alberta Government—a millennium award for distinguished citizens of Alberta, to commemorate the Millennium year 2005.

Theatre 100 awarded to **"100 theatre practitioners in Alberta for outstanding contribution to the development of theatre in the last 100 years."** Awarded in 2006, but still, a millennium award.

Down Town Heroes awarded in 2009 by the city of Grande Prairie to fifty citizens for the contribution to the cultural development of the city. This was to celebrate the 50th anniversary of the city.

Instructor Emeritus of Grande Prairie Regional College. Awarded in 2008.

The Rock awarded in 2009 by the college community—an annual award for distinguished services to Grande Prairie Regional College.

IMAGES

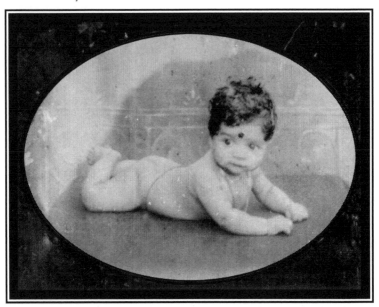

Author circa 1929

Author's parents: Mr. Parameswaran Nair and Mrs. Jagadamma

Author's in-laws: Mr. Keshavlal Oza and Mrs. Savitri Oza

*The Lord Chamberlain is
commanded by Her Majesty to invite*

Mrs N. S. Nayar

*to a Reception at Buckingham Palace
on Monday, the 9th July 1962, from 6 to 8 o'clock p. m.*

*An answer is requested addressed to
The Lord Chamberlain,
St. James's Palace, S.W.1.*

Dress: National Dress or Lounge Suit.

Invitation to tea at Buckingham Palace

Author's family: wife Nalini, son Nikku and daughter Radha

Author as Sir Peter Teazle in *The School for Scandal*, 1954

Author performing live for Uganda TV, 1964

Author and wife on the Southern Hemipshere and
friend Patrick Lobo on the Northern Hemisphere, 1963

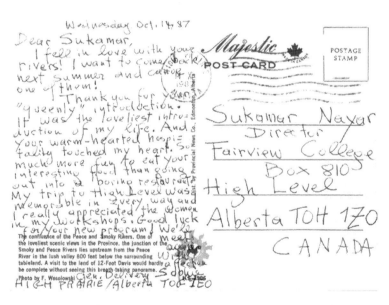

Letter from Dr. Sophie Freud, granddaughter of
Dr. Sigmund Freud, dated 1987

Author with Constantin Skvortsov at Boris
Pasternak's grave in Moscow, 2000

Author with Dr. Dubov and family in Vladimir, Russia, 2001

Directing *Children of a Lesser God*, 1989

Author as Victor Velasco in *Barefoot in the Park*, 1997

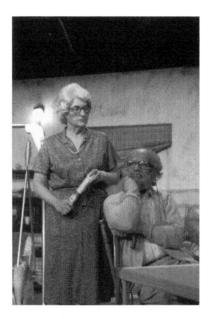

Author as Weller Martin in *The Gin Game,* 1986

Consulting with choreographer Marie Nychka,
Jesus Christ Superstar, 2006

GRANDE PRAIRIE LIVE THEATRE

'ART'

by
Yasmina Reza

Translated by
Christopher Hampton

Producer / Director
SUKUMAR NAYAR

Starring
Harold Friesen, Liam McGowan, Glenn Rogers
SECOND STREET THEATRE
February 10 - 11 - 12 - 17 - 18 - 19 - 24 - 25 - 26, 2005
7:00 p.m.

Alberta
Foundation
for the Arts

ticket information
538.1616

SECOND STREET
THEATRE

From the Director archives